Tea and Chinese Culture

Tea and Chinese Culture

By Ling Wang

LONG RIVER PRESS
San Francisco

Copyright © 2005 Long River Press
First Edition 2005
Editors: Luo Tianyou, Xu Rong
Designer: Liu Guihong

The publisher gratefully acknowledges the following individvals and agencies who have contributed illustrations for this volume: China Pictorial, Foreign Languages Press, Geng Zhuo, Hu Xiaoqi, Li Chunsheng, Liu Guihong, Wang Huimin, and many others.

Library of Congress Cataloging-in-Publication Data

Wang, Ling.
  [Chinese tea culture]
  Tea and Chinese culture / by Ling Wang.
      p. cm.
  Originally published: Chinese tea culture. Beijing : Foreign Language
Press, 2000.
  ISBN 1-59265-025-2
  1. Tea--China--History. 2. China--Social life and customs. I. Title.
GT2907.C6W335 2005
394.1'2--dc22
                        2004015185

Published in the United States of America by
Long River Press
San Francisco, CA 94080
Printed in China
10 9 8 7 6 5 4 3 2 1

Date-flowers fall in showers on my hooded head.
At both ends of the village wheels are spinning thread.
A straw-cloaked man sells cucumber beneath a willow tree.

Wine-drowsy when the road is long, I yawn for bed.
Throat parched when sun is high, I long for tea.
I'll knock at this door. What have they for me?

—Su Dongpo, Song Dynasty

Contents

Introduction

Tea has played an important role in the social and cultural fabric of life around the world for thousands of years. It has captivated the attention of artists, writers, philosophers, and people from every section of society. It is enjoyed for its health benefits and its contribution to living a better, simpler, and aesthetically appealing life. Today, tea continues to be one of the world's most popular beverages, enjoying renewed popularity with each new generation who discovers its wonderful gifts.

An old Chinese adage goes:

When we rise in the morning, the ready our daily firewood, rice, cooking oil, salt, soy, vinegar, and tea.

Whenever friends and family sit around a table, a cup of fragrant tea will lend its rich aroma and warm presence to any occasion. In ancient times, many Chinese, including emperors and common people alike, were captivated by its unique fragrance and aesthetic experience. During the Qing Dynasty, for example, Emperor Kangxi, who reigned from 1662 to 1722, arrived at Taihu Lake in Suzhou on his third inspection tour of the regions south of the Yangtze River. There, he was offered a cup of tea called, "Xia Sha Ren Xiang (Astounding Fragrance)." After drinking it, the Emperor thought that while the tea had a pleasant taste, its name was not particularly elegant. The Emperor, having been told that this particular tea was harvested during the spring months from the slopes of Biluo mountain, chose

 The Book of Tea

🍵 *Portrait of Emperor Kangxi*

to rename it *Biluochun* (literally, Biluo in Spring).

Many years later, the grandson of Emperor Kangxi, Emperor Qianlong, who reigned from 1736 to 1795, was also a devoted disciple of tea. During the first lunar month of each new year, the Emperor would hold festive tea parties: sampling various teas while composing poems honoring the occasion. Such occasions were some of the finest and most rarefied forms of art and culture in China's imperial age.

Although many nations have produced tea in an astonishing array of varieties, the name of China is generally synonymous with this fascinating beverage throughout the world. When did China first discover tea and its various uses? According to an ancient text called *Shen Nong Ben Cao Jing* (Shen Nong's Herbal Classic), dating from some 2,700 years ago, people were often poisoned by eating some of the various wild herbs they had picked. Shen Nong, a legendary figure also known as Yan Di, or, the Holy Farmer, is credited with inventing the plough and was one of the first to discover the medicinal properties of various types of plants.

The tea plant, originally used as a medicinal herb, possessed the ability to detoxify and reinvigorate those who used it. The evolution from medicinal herb to favored drink took another step in 59 B.C., when the writer Wang Bao mentioned in his work, entitled "A Contract with a Servant," that the servant should boil tea for his master and go to Wuyang (located in Sichuan Province, then a famous tea producing region) to buy tea. This written record reveals that tea, as a drink, emerged

🍵 *Shen Nong Ben Cao Jing*

no later than the Western Han Period (ca. 206B.C. – A.D. 23).

During the Three Kingdoms Period (220-280), the King of the State of Wu, Sun Hao (242-283), ordered his ministers to drink liquor each time he entertained them, thus gaining amusement from their drunkenness. A minister named Wei Yao could not drink, however, so Sun Hao gave him tea secretly instead of liquor. From that episode, the drinking of tea began to gain favor among the gentry elite.

During the Northern and Southern dynasties (420-589), Buddhism gained popularity and monks refreshed themselves with tea after meditation. Drinking tea became a widespread practice in temples big and small throughout the countryside. Tea was even grown alongside the temples and harvested by the monks themselves, who studied and mastered the various characteristics of tea in all its forms and varieties. This development marked the philosophic and aesthetic integration of tea with Buddhism.

In the Tang Dynasty (618-907), China's glorious golden age of art and culture, tea drinking achieved even greater popularity. Since tea could stimulate the brain, scholars took delight in its inspirational properties, composing poems and painting pictures with tea as the central theme. At that time, tea was grown mainly in Sichuan, Hunan, Hubei, Jiangxi, and Fujian provinces, and volume of the tea trade grew exponentially. Noted Tang poet Bai Juyi wrote:

The businessman stressed profits

He belittled the affection for his wife.

The month before last he went to Fuliang to buy tea.

Lu Yu (733-804), perhaps more than anyone else summed up the experience of the then extant tea culture most succinctly when he wrote *The Book of Tea*, known to be the earliest treatise on tea ever published. In his work, Lu Yu systematically related the origins

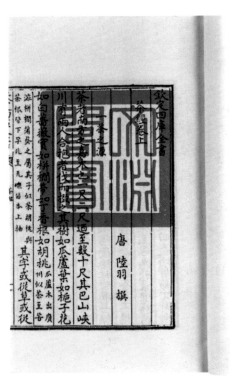

🌸 *The Book of Tea (Qing Dynasty Copy)*

of tea, together with information about its natural history, methods of cultivation, and techniques of harvesting. Lu Yu went on to describe the processes of producing tea, including ceremonial and aesthetic aspects of tea such as preparation, brewing, steeping, and drinking, as well as the variety of tea vessels used.

During the Song (960-1279) and Yuan (1271-1368) dynasties, a popular custom was the "appraisal" of tea, which could only be accomplished by using tea of the highest grade. Somewhat similar to the process of contemporary wine tasting in the Western world, the appraisal of tea considered various aspects of tea making such as the use of water, tea vessels, and the various colors and aromas of tea. Tea appraisals also often blended with meditation or contemplation, with scholars or artists musing on the creative or inspirational effects of a particular type of tea. Rather than drinking liquor, which often rendered one intoxicated, tea stimulated the creative and inspirational energies of the mind, taking scholars and artists to new levels of observation and expression.

4

Drinking tea was thus not only for the quenching of one's thirst, but became a pastime and a means of relaxation. In addition, tea drinking inspired many types of cultural activities. For example, poems and paintings inspired by tea, as well as songs, dances, and local operas about tea, which together show the close relationship between tea and Chinese aesthetics as developing into an almost spiritual experience.

🔹 *Sichuan village teahouse scene*

The various folk customs of tea drinking reflected the Chinese people's interest in tea culture. A typical example of this could be found in the teahouses dotting the streets and lanes of Chinese cities and villages. People of all social classes, from the gentry elite to common people alike, enjoyed the pastime of tea drinking and liked to gather together at tea houses. Business was conducted, ideas were exchanged, and strangers became friends. Even personal disputes were judged and mediated in the pleasant, soothing atmosphere of the teahouse. Teahouses were also places where people could enjoy entertainment, such as traditional opera and storytelling. They could be loud, at times boisterous places, or small, quiet, and intimate spaces. It can truly be said that teahouses reflected the social life of China in cross section, as well as serving as the

🌸 *Lao She teahouse (Beijing)*

political, economic and cultural center for the population. Some of the most famous teahouses in China include the Lao She Teahouse in Beijing, the Taotaoju Teahouse in Guangzhou, and the Bayu Teahouse in Chongqing. In Guangzhou, China's bustling southern metropolis, people go to teahouses every day, enjoying tea together with light snacks and other refreshments. In Sichuan, people can relax on rows of bamboo chairs, drinking tea while talking about all manner of subjects. The teahouses in Beijing have a rich cultural flavor reflecting the history and political and academic traditions of modern China.

People often used tea as a betrothal gift, for it was said that tea could not be "transplanted." After accepting tea as a betrothal gift, for example, a girl could not capriciously change her decision to marry her fiancé. According to a line of dialogue in the well-known Chinese novel *Hong Lou Meng* (A Dream of Red Mansions), written by Cao Xueqin during the Qing Dynasty, the character of Wang Xifeng spoke these words to the character of Lin Daiyu:

Since you have drunk our tea, why not become our sister-in-law?

Serving tea to entertain guests is one of the most fundamental types of social behavior in China, and an ideal way to learn more about the social interaction of its people. A famous poem goes:

A guest came to my home on a cold night.

Hastily I made tea in lieu of wine.

Atop the bamboo stove, water boiled in the kettle above the red flame.

Looking through the window, the moon was made more beautiful by plum trees in blossom.

🌸 *Lin Daiyu*

Prior to the Tang Dynasty, Chinese tea was exported by land and sea, first to Japan and

Tea and Chinese Culture

Korea, then to India and Central Asia, and, in the Ming and Qing dynasties, to the middle East, Africa, and the Arabian peninsula. In the early part of the 17th century, Chinese tea was exported to Europe, where European aristocracy embraced tea drinking as a high cultural art. Today, tea has become the most popular drink consumed throughout the world. The output of tea from India, China, and Sri Lanka (Ceylon) alone constitutes over 60 percent of the world's total. Like Chinese silk and porcelain, Chinese tea has made an immeasurably significant contribution to world history.

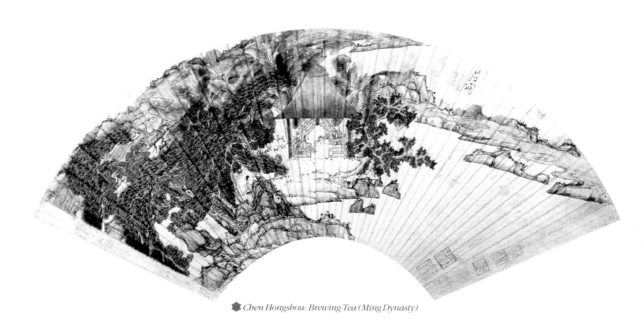

Chen Hongshou: Brewing Tea (Ming Dynasty)

Wen Zhenming: *Tasting Tea (detail), Ming Dynasty*

Chapter 1

1. The Origins of Tea

The discovery and use of tea in China can be traced back to the legendary tale of Yan Di, also known as Shen Nong, the Holy Farmer, and one of the "Three August (majestic) Ones." Yan Di invented the plough and discovered the medicinal virtues of plants. The Chinese people often refer to themselves as descendants of Yan Di as well as Huang Di, the Yellow Emperor.

China is a land where scientific and technological innovation in the agricultural sciences were highly advanced at a very early period in history when compared with other emerging or developing civilizations. Yan Di was said to have invented many farm tools and taught people how to grow crops effectively.

Yan Di is also known as the "God of Medicine" in Chinese legend for his ability to select and combine various wild plants and herbs for apothecary and medicinal properties. Fearless, he tasted wild plants and herbs himself to discover their effects on the human body.

During the course of his research, Yan Di discovered the tea plant, brewed the leaves in hot water in a ceramic urn, and then proceeded to sip the hot liquid. Almost immediately, he felt a sense of purification, as if the toxins in his body were magically evaporating. Since those ancient times, it is said in popular legend, Chinese people have regarded tea as an integral part of their health and well-being.

🍵 *Yan Di*

Early in the Zhou (Chou) Dynasty (c. 11th century B.C.-771 B.C.), tea was used for medicinal remedies by all people from commoners to the noblest families. The people of Sichuan, for example, paid a tribute of tea to Emperor Wu of the Zhou Dynasty. In *The Ritual of Zhou,* an ancient historical text, for example, there are numerous records concerning the protocol involving the use of tea in the royal court dating from 3,000 years ago.

🍵 *Celadon tea ware, Han Dynasty (detail)*

By the Han Dynasty (206 B.C. – A.D. 220), the growth and harvesting of tea had grown tremendously, laying the foundation for its wide, almost universal use throughout China in later historical periods. Tea itself had evolved greatly during this period. No longer used only as a medicinal drink, tea was soon to become the preferred beverage of society. Boxes of tea have been found in Han tombs built during the 2nd century B.C., which show that even in the early Han era, noble families relied heavily on tea and considered it important enough to be placed in tombs for use in the afterlife.

11

The art of tea drinking is said to have originated in the company of scholars, and was first formally recorded in an essay written by Wang Bao in 59 B.C. entitled "A Contract with a Servant." In the Han Dynasty, there was a man named Wang Ziyuan in Sichuan who traveled to Chengdu to take a civil service examination. In Chengdu, he arrived at the house of his friend only to discover that he had recently passed away. His friend's widow, Yang Hui, still lived there with her young servant. Perhaps Yang Hui adored Wang Ziyuan, for she received him warmly, and allowed her servant, named Bian Liao, to serve tea to Wang as if he were master of the house.

🍵 *A Contract with a Servant*

Unhappy with this situation, the loyal Bian Liao ran to his late master's tomb, complaining tearfully: "My good Master, I look after your house but I will not look after your wife's lover!" Learning of Bian Liao's unhappiness, Yang Hui and Wang Ziyuan at first became very angry. They decided, however, that their only recourse was to offer Bian Liao 15,000 coins in exchange for him formally becoming Wang's servant. Wang drew up a formal contract which stipulated what Bian Liao should do every day, including buying tea at Wuyang Market, brewing tea with the utmost care, then carefully cleaning and putting away the tea sets. The details of Wang's contract show the extent to which scholars will go to ensure their tea drinking ritual remains an important part of everyday life.

Zhuge Liang, Prime Minister of the State of Shu during the Three Kingdoms Period, is known to almost every household in China. Zhuge's wisdom and decision-making in civil and military affairs are still studied and respected by later generations. Tradition credits Zhuge Liang with popularizing tea cultivation in Yunnan Province. Zhuge Liang is also known by the name of Kongming, and people from Yunnan Province to this day refer to the tea plant as a "Kongming Tree."

Zhuge Liang

Why was the drinking of tea so attractive to China's scholarly class? In part, it was because so many scholars and writers drew their inspiration from drinking tea, as they sat in silent contemplation of beautiful far-off mountains, green forests, or calming waters. In this way the tea served to soothe both body and spirit, helping along the philosophical and spiritual quest for knowledge and understanding. It would be accurate to say that the spirit of the tea blended perfectly with the aesthetic sensibilities of the scholarly class.

In the Han Dynasty, Chinese rulers advocated thrift. In the early Western Han Dynasty, for example, the Emperor rode in a simple ox cart and did not take to ornate carriages or other means of transport readily. In the Eastern Han Dynasty (25-220), the economy thrived but cultural relations and the societal code of ethics still advocated filial piety, friendship, honesty, and moral and social uprightness. Even some officials were incorruptible and thrifty, reflecting the simple and friendly virtues of the Chinese people from time immemorial.

However, in the Eastern and Western Jin dynasties (265-420) and the Northern and Southern dynasties period, the social landscape of China changed suddenly. Nobles and gentry elite competed against each other in bold displays of extravagance. In the Jin Dynasty, for example, an official named He Zeng went even further than the Emperor by living extravagantly with expensive robes, ornate chariots, and seemingly endless amounts of food. He Zeng spent 10,000 coins a day on food, while his son spent 20,000 coins. Not to be outdone, Ren Kai, a very wealthy nobleman, spent 20,000 coins on every meal! Another nobleman, Shi Chong, enjoyed rare delicacies from land and sea at each meal, and was always accompanied by at least ten servants.

In the Southern Dynasty, Emperor Liangwu (502-550) was thrifty, while his brother, Xiao Hong, lived in luxury. Xiao Hong was reported to have built many private storehouses—their contents unknown. Emperor Liangwu went to investigate, fearing that his brother was hoarding weapons for a possible coup. Instead of weapons, what Liangwu found in the storehouses were innumerable treasures collected from all parts of the empire. Such excess worried responsible, sober-minded rulers who advocated moral cultivation and incorruptibility above all other virtues. As it turns out, tea would play a major role in this campaign.

Tea represents purity. It takes root in the bosoms of hills and valleys, and absorbs rain and dew in high mountains in order to grow green leaves. Tea blossoms beautifully in the glow of dawn and dusk. In ancient China, people believed that tea should never be transplanted, and because of this trait, tea was praised for its tenacity. It exhibits characteristics of both luxury and strength.

Lu Na, an official of the Eastern Jin Dynasty, was incorruptible. As chief of prefecture, he would not accept a salary. Later, the imperial court recalled him and appointed him to the position of Left Service Official. When his family asked him how many boats of treasure were to be loaded, he answered that he wanted only the grain needed on the journey. When Lu Na acted as head of Wuxing prefecture, a well-known senior general, Xie An, planned to visit him. Lu Na's nephew thought that such a noble guest should be treated with consideration. When he saw that his uncle had not yet made any preparations, he decided to act on his own.

After Xie An arrived, Lu Na served him only tea and fruit. Seeing this, Lu Na's nephew gave a grand banquet out of fear of appearing to neglect the guest. After Xia An left, Lu Na told his nephew resentfully, "You did not win honor for me, but just smeared my clean virtue."

In the Southern and Northern dynasties period, some emperors drank tea instead of liquor as a means of expressing their simple disposition and thrift ways. In the Southern Qi Dynasty, Emperor Shizu was a particularly enlightened ruler. During the decade of his reign there were almost no military conflicts, and the populace lived and prospered in peace—building families and strengthening the economy. The Emperor dismissed wanton amusement as too excessive and wasteful of the people. When the Emperor knew that he was dying, he issued an edict proclaiming that his funeral should not be extravagant and a burden on the resources of the common people. The Emperor said that at his funeral only several plates of cooked rice and fruit and a cup of tea rather than the traditional "three sacrifices" (three domestic animals, i.e. cattle, sheep and pigs, used as sacrificial offerings) would be offered. In addition, he ordered that from that time on, anyone, be they nobility or commoner, should abide by such a rule. The Emperor's wishes set a precedent: as tea soon began to be used as a sacrificial offering to follow the Emperor's example of thrift, purity, and simplicity.

Prior to the emergence of the Southern and Northern dynasties, China faced the ravages of war. The north was in chaos while the south remained relatively peaceful and untouched by military conflict. It was in this environment where scholars often gathered and held "cultural salons," discussing literature, philosophy, and other subjects at their whim. Many of the intellectual class enjoyed liquor, and often drank as they discussed or contemplated together alongside clean waters and green hills.

In subsequent years, however, scholars began to switch from liquor to tea. There were two main reasons: prolonged drinking of liquor was determined to be detrimental to one's health and well being, and the fact that high quality liquor could be acquired only by the most affluent individuals. Therefore, tea soon gained favor. If the "cultivation of incorruptibility" associated with tea and advocated by Lu Na, Huan Wen (a statesman with considerable military ability in Lu Na's time), and others who advocated the drinking of tea instead of liquor symbolized the spirit of tea, the use of tea by scholars to keep sober and inspire their thinking reflected the direct effect of tea on the popular psyche of the people.

During the Southern and Northern dynasties, known to history as a period of cultural exchange, Taoist metaphysics gained immense popularity as a subject of discussion. Taoism is one of the earliest indigenous philosophies to have been formed in China. Essentially a complex set of relationships between the human and natural world, elements of traditional Taoism (such as the *Dao De Jing*) were blended with the social and ethical tenets of Confucianism, giving rise to a new popular ethos. The followers of metaphysics emphasized family, deportment, and high ethics. They also advocated free form thought and proposed profound theories on nature and natural law—such as the relationship between all living things. There were talks and lectures, some lasting for hours, and many times with hundreds, even thousands of audience members listening in rapt attention. In situations such as these, tea became indispensable: its material and spiritual effects were perfectly unified with the Taoist discussions. Thus, tea culture was imbued with the mysterious flavor of Chinese philosophy.

 15

The oldest spiritual principle in China is Taoism, which enjoys a much longer history than Confucianism or Buddhism. While not a religion *per se*, Taoism is a school of thought based on the writings of Laozi (Lao Tzu), and takes its form as a system of beliefs which hold that man is an integral part of nature, while emphasizing the harmonious relationship between man, nature, and the universe. Taoism advocated overcoming one's mortal failings by tapping into special resources through the training of one's body and mind. The Chinese people refer to those who have succeeded in practicing extreme acts of asceticism or self-sacrifice as "immortals," and believe that they possess both special wisdom and miraculous powers. Such individuals are revered rather than worshipped, and are held in high esteem by the Chinese people.

Laozi (Lao Tzu)

With the spread of Buddhism

from India into China, it was at first taken for granted that Buddhist and Taoist "immortals" were alike in how they sat in meditation. Thus, Buddhist figures came to be known as "immortals" as well. Despite the philosophical contrasts between Taoist, Confucian, and Buddhist practices, all relied on tea and tea drinking in the discussion and promotion of their respective ideas within society.

Monk brewing tea

Many classical works of Chinese history and literature featured stories about immortals and tea. During the reign of Emperor Yuandi in the Jin Dynasty, for example, there was an elderly woman who often sold tea at the local market. Though the tea was pouring from morning until night, her kettle was always full. The elderly woman even helped the poor by using the income she received from the sale of tea. Local authorities, however, were displeased and put her into prison. But at night the merciful old woman flew away—with her tea sets in tow—from the window of the prison. It was a widely held belief that ancient immortals could fly, so the old woman was immediately thought to be one of the Taoist immortals.

Other historical texts relate the story of a monk named Fa Yao, who lived in the time of the Southern Dynasty, and who greatly enjoyed the drinking of tea. Fa Yao reportedly died at the age of 99. His impressive age was attributed to the magical properties of tea. Thus, even a man of advanced years was treated as if he were an immortal, since it was believed that in ancient times living conditions were harsh, so it was considered extremely rare for anyone to attain such an impressive life span.

Why did the Chinese people connect tea with their belief in the legend of the immortals? According to Taoist theory, human vitality lies within collateral channels. Tea acts as a filter—absorbing impurities while helping to dredge or clear away these channels of energy. In addition, tea, which could allow one to relax without feeling the ill effects of intoxication, was deemed a necessity to the practice of Taoism or Buddhism, since both advocated sitting in meditation. Thus, the effect of tea drinking was connected with the oldest Chinese philosophy, including its rules of keeping and maintaining good health, together with a personal elevation within the greater spiritual sphere.

Tea has survived more than 3,000 years and continues to thrive today. From the Han Dynasty, tea has been planted and used formally in great abundance in China. Owing to its unique properties and its spiritual effect on the mind and body. It has received the praise of scholars, literary figures, the ruling class, and the common people. Its sweet scent, mild taste, and rich fragrance have captivated people from all walks of life.

🍵 *Tea as medicinal herb*

However, before the Han Dynasty, the spiritual and cultural effects of tea were not catalogued in great detail. The way of drinking tea had not yet emerged as an art form, nor did it form into a cohesive philosophy or systematic set of rules that would have enlightened people's thoughts and emotions on a truly large scale. Early Chinese tea culture was embryonic from the time of the Han Dynasty—when tea drinking formally appeared in historical records—to the Southern and Northern dynasties, when tea was widely used by scholars and philosophers.

In subsequent dynasties, the real emergence of tea culture as a high art form would come into being.

🍵 *Tea cup made of zisha (Ming Dynasty)*

Most teas can be served on any occasion and with almost any type of food. However, the following are known to be especially good combinations:

Green Tea: With salty foods and some desserts.

White Tea: After a heavy meal to stimulate digestion.

Black Tea: After oily or greasy food.

Red Tea: With sweet desserts.

Oolong Tea (esp. Ti Kwan Yin): After seafood.

Jasmine Tea: After strong or spicy food.

Chapter 2

2. Tea Culture in Dynastic China

Chinese tea culture as we know it today took its initial shape during the Tang Dynasty, during what is typically referred to as the Golden Age of Chinese art and culture. The economic prosperity, social, and cultural enlightenment in terms of music and art, together with ever increasing trade and foreign exchanges along the Silk Road, provided a rich environment for the blossoming of tea culture in the Tang.

During the period that the tea plant was cultivated in over 40 prefectures, which comprised the Tang empire, the practice of tea drinking had extended into people's daily lives. Emperors of the later Tang, who were especially fond of tea, ordered tea-producing areas to send their first crop, which was usually considered the best, directly to the palace, where a grand banquet was held each Spring in honor of the Qing Ming (Pure Brightness) Festival, which marked the beginning of the 5th solar term, usually occurring in early April. During this time, many people worship at their ancestral graves. Many officials even received a promotion for paying a tribute to the Emperor in the form of tea, which in turn inspired the satirical poem:

The father wins promotion through tea, which also brings the son riches. Why don't other intellectuals take this route instead of studying the "Spring and Autumn Annals" and "A Horseback Diagram from the Yellow River?"

🏮 *Imperial concubines and the "tea game"*

To win the Emperor's approval, imperial concubines thought of ways to improve upon the art of making

Imperial concubines and the "tea game"

tea and drinking tea, and gradually developed a type of tea drinking game. In the Tang Dynasty, intellectuals aiming to secure official positions had to undertake the grueling system of imperial examinations, the final of which was held in the Tang capital and directly presided over by the Emperor. In the examination, supervised by many court officials, candidates were kept isolated in what often resembled wooden outhouses to avoid cheating, and were only allowed to take in a small amount of solid food. The only exception to this rule was tea, which could be sent to each candidate for their refreshment. Princes and ministers, following the example of the Emperor, took pride in their appreciation for tea. Li Deyu, the grand councilor, even went so far as to use the finest spring water from a region thousands of miles away, just to make a pot of tea.

🍵 *Tang Dynasty art*

Drinking tea for relaxation and as a social activity was practiced initially by intellectuals, and the art of tea drinking as well as the craft of composing poetry while drinking tea flourished during the Tang Dynasty. The use of liquor had previously helped to encourage and inspire poets, but in the Tang, alcohol was officially prohibited because it required the use of too much grain to produce. Consequently, alcohol production was greatly reduced. By contrast, tea offered a far less expensive solution, and soon began to supplant alcohol as drink for refined tastes. At the time Buddhism was flourishing, and monks in temples were required to sit in meditation in the evening without taking their supper. But many young, less experienced monks found this difficult, so the Lingyan Temple at Mount Tai made an exception, allowing the monks to have tea during the evening meditation. Not

🍵*Jianzhen, a buddhist monk of the Tang Dynasty*

surprisingly, the monks discovered the calming effects of tea, but also the way in which it improved their concentration and focus. It was not long before this practice spread throughout the entire country, where it eventually became an accepted practice.

Tea also became a form of sacrifice to the Buddha as well as a special drink served to distinguished visitors. Because of the large, sustained demand for tea, temples began to grow tea plants on their own. Coincidentally, due to their mountainous location, and exposure to rainfall and sunshine, tea produced by temple monks was of unusually high quality. With the popularity of drinking tea firmly entrenched among ordinary people, tea shops soon appeared in cities and towns across the countryside, even in the central provinces such as Shandong, Hunan, and Shanxi, where tea production was historically low by comparison.

The tea trade, a useful means for the Tang Dynasty to increase state revenue, was also established to promote geographic, economic, and cultural exchanges with neighboring ethnic groups. Bartering tea for horses, for example, was very common in border areas at the time. The Tang people's universal love for tea also gave the impetus for further research into the history of tea. Historically, ten main functions of tea were summarized thusly:

1. Tea is beneficial to health and able to dredge clear the body's channels, relieving headaches and fatigue.
2. Tea can help dispel the effects of alcohol.
3. Tea, when dressed with sauces, can serve as nourishing "porridge" to allay hunger.
4. Tea can help drive away summer heat.
5. Tea can help shake off drowsiness.
6. Tea can help to purify the spirit and eliminate anxiety.
7. Tea can aid in the digestion of food.
8. Tea can be used to eliminate toxins from the body.
9. Tea is conducive to longevity
10. Tea can invigorate the body and inspire the mind.

The Chinese people attach the same importance to the quality of their material and spiritual lives. For instance, they eat and drink to satisfy their physiological requirements, and to refresh and inspire their minds as well. Drinking alcohol, always regarded as proper etiquette at banquets and official ceremonies, is also a customary practice for soldiers who are about to go into battle as a display of heroism. Chinese people are very particular about the aroma, color, and taste of their food, which are taken not only to fill the stomach, but are also viewed as objects with aesthetic value.

It seems only natural that tea, a drink especially valued among intellectuals, became a material and aesthetic pursuit replete with cultural and ideological meaning. It was the Tang people who further developed the art of making and drinking tea, imbuing the whole process with the rhyme of a poem and making the drinker meditate on the philosophy of life. Not surprisingly, Lu Yu, author of *The Book of Tea* and the first person who systematically laid down the procedural and aesthetic foundations for the tea ceremony and the promotion of tea culture, is referred to as the patron saint of tea in Chinese history.

Lu Yu, born at Jingling, Fuzhou (present-day Tianmen County in Hubei Province), lived during the Tang's flourishing ages of Kaiyuan and Tianbao. An orphan abandoned by his parents, Lu Yu was taken in by Ji Gong, an eminent Buddhist monk, and brought up in a temple named Longgai. Ji Gong loved tea very much and grew many tea plants around the temple. Little Lu Yu learned many arts of culti-vating and making tea from Ji Gong, and, with time, gradually became an expert himself. Ac-cording to legend, once when Ji Gong was called to lecture on the teachings of Buddha at the im-perial court, he felt quite disappointed with the tea served there. But one day he was suddenly overjoyed after taking several sips of tea, exclaiming, "Ah! It's made by my disciple Lu Yu!" Ji Gong had indeed spoken the truth, for Lu Yu had been specially summoned to make tea for him.

🍵 *Lu Yu*

Although he grew up in a Buddhist temple, Lu Yu was more interested in Confucianism. The reclusive life in a lonely temple was too much for him. He eventually left to join a theatrical troupe. As he was clever, he not only acted but also wrote many humorous plays. Later he won the recognition of Li Qiwu, the prefect of Jingling, who helped him to go to nearby Mount Tianmen to learn Confucian teachings from an old scholar. But the good times did not last long. Lu Yu's study was interrupted by An Lushan's revolt in the north, which drove the Emperor Tang Xuanzong south to Sichuan from the capital Chang'an. Lu Yu was forced to go with the fugitives to Huzhou, a tea-growing area in the south. There he collected much useful information about the cultivation, harvesting, and preparation of tea, and also made friends with some of the most famous poets, monks, calligraphers, and statesmen of the period through their mutual love of tea. On the basis of profound discussions with his friends on the art of making and drinking tea, together with his own long-term explorations of tea culture, Lu Yu wrote *The Book of Tea*, the first treatise on tea and tea culture in the world.

The Book of Tea is not only a treatise on tea, but also a reflective synthesis of natural and social sciences and the material and ideological world. It creates an art form out of the process of drinking tea, including its baking, water selection, use and display of tea sets, and, of course, drinking, all of which are imbued with a unique aesthetic approach. Lu Yu held that people who loved drinking tea should excel in virtue. He emphasized the golden mean of Confucianism, the perseverance of Buddhists in seeking truth, and the Taoists' theory that man is an integral part of nature. In Lu Yu's world, these characteristics all blend together harmoniously in the process of enjoying tea. *The Book of Tea* is regarded as the authoritative summary of Chinese tea culture before the mid-Tang period. Later Tang thinkers continued to write new works on tea culture, such as *Sixteen Varieties of Tea* by Su Yi, which added new ideas to the art of tea culture,

The Book of Tea (Japanese Copy)

and *Comments on the Waters for Making Tea* by Zhang Youxin, which detailed the value of the water in the rivers, springs, pools, and lakes throughout China. Liu Zhenliang, a palace eunuch who had reached a high level of attainment in tea culture, continued to expand on the ten traditional virtues of tea.

Despite their considerable knowledge, however, these thinkers were only standing on the shoulders of Lu Yu, who has even been referred to as the God of Tea, a great honor indeed, since the concept of Gods in Chinese myth and legend were perceived as the living spirits of great mortal people. Lu Yu, an eminent contributor to the culture of tea, was undoubtedly worthy of the title.

In the Tang Dynasty, the habit of drinking tea spread from the imperial court to towns and the countryside; and it was the literati, scholars, and Buddhist monks who played a leading role in the advocacy of tea culture. But things changed in the Song Dynasty, when the influence of intellectuals on the culture of tea gradually weakened. Although many famous literati, such as Su Shi, the great writer of the Northern Song, Li Qingzhao, the celebrated female poet, and Lu You, a prolific poet of the Southern Song, were fond of tea and wrote many highly influential poems, they contributed little to the construction of tea culture in popular society. Tea culture at that time was expanded and publicized by two seemingly opposite strengths—that is, the imperial court, and the ordinary people.

🍵 *Su Dongpo*

Emperors of the Song Dynasty possessed a special love of tea, and some of them were avid followers of the tea ceremony in all its myriad and intricate details. Emperor Song Huizong even wrote a treatise on tea, entitled *A Grand View on Tea*. Because of the supreme standing of the Emperor, the natural and artistic qualities of tea given as tribute to the imperial court were very seriously studied by all those who had any association with tea or tea making.

🍵 *Emperor Huizong, Song Dynasty*

For ease of measurement, transport, and storage, it had been a common practice to compress processed tea leaves into cake form. When tea culture was in bloom, the Song people, in order to add to the beauty of tea, began to make such cakes in a more ingenious way, such as having the imperial dragon or phoenix design embossed on them. Such tea, paid as a tribute to the Emperor, was produced mainly in Jianzhou prefecture by two famous officials, Ding Wei and Cai Xiang.

🌸 *Tea cakes in the shape of dragons (Song Dynasty)*

Jianzhou, a prefecture originally called Jian'an, was located in present-day Fujian Province. A place with beautiful scenery and many Buddhist temples, it had a flourishing tea cultivation program, and had been designated to produce tea cakes for the court even before the Song Dynasty.

During the reign of Song Emperor Taizong, Ding Wei was the superintendent of imperial tea production in Jianzhou. A talented man, Ding Wei excelled at writing poems, painting, playing Chinese chess, and appreciating music, as well as being well versed in Buddhist and Taoist teachings. To win the Emperor's favor, or a higher position and better salary, Ding

Wei undertook an effort to create new styles of tea cakes. During the Tang Dynasty, for instance, the cakes had a hole in the middle for a string to run through to hold them together. Consequently, the cakes were very roughly made and their appearance suggested utility rather than aesthetic beauty. Ding Wei ceased to produce the cakes with holes in them, and designed many new patterns and designs for tea cake production.

Cai Xiang, a man of letters, and also one of the finest calligraphers of the time, had different rules of conduct from those of Ding Wei, who liked to humor the Emperor. Cai Xiang often would remonstrate the Emperor, suggesting he live a simple life while demonstrating more solicitude for the ordinary people. During his two tenures as the Magistrate of Fuzhou, he had done the local people a lot of good, building up sea walls, irrigating farms, and planting pine trees along roads for hundreds of miles to protect them from dust and erosion. Noble and unsullied, he demonstrated the virtue of a true tea scholar. He once wrote his own treatise on tea, the first part of which described the criteria for judging the quality of tea: the color, fragrance, and taste. The latter part concerned tea sets, especially the harmony between the colors of the pottery and the tea itself. Cai Xiang also made contributions to the production of tea cakes by shaping them into figures of dragons.

Differing from ordinary tea products, tea cakes in the shape of dragons and phoenixes demonstrated artistry and unique cultural features heretofore not seen on anything as ubiquitous as a tea cake. In fact, it was quite complicated to make such tribute tea, for the tea leaves had to be picked at dawn before the Grain Rain (the 6th solar term, falling in late April), and carefully selected, steamed, pressed, ground, caked, baked, and packed, before being sent to the Emperor. Some pattern dies, one inch in diameter, were used to make only 100 tea cakes every year. It goes without saying such tea cakes were luxuriously packed, first in the leaves of a special kind of tree, then in layers of yellow silk, then in red laquerware cases with gold padlocks and official red seals, and finally in special bamboo outer cases.

Such tribute tea, called "Bird-Tongue Bud," could have at most three buds on each leaf. According to contemporary records, one cake of such tea had a value of 400,000 copper coins at the time. These expensive teas could only be enjoyed by the Emperor, his empress, and concubines. The palace officials, if they happened to be awarded one such cake by the Emperor, would never actually use it to make tea but instead view it as a gift of the highest order.

Ouyang Xiu, a celebrated member of the literati and statesman of the Song Dynasty, was granted only one such tea cake during his twenty years of service at the imperial court; and it was almost impossible for ordinary people to even have a look at it. Such luxurious practices deviated from the spirit of tea culture and the rule of simplicity originally advocated by Lu Yu and practiced by many others. On the other hand, such products showed the great inspiration and attention to detail of the craftsmen who made tea cakes of such rare and refined quality.

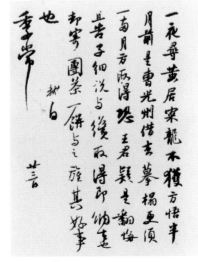

🍵 *Tea cakes as a gift (Su Shi)*

29

In China, there existed a group activity in which people could compare and place value upon the quality of different teas. By the Tang Dynasty, the practice, commonly called the "tea competition," was an activity of the wealthy class, but by the Song Dynasty it was common to all social strata.

The tea competition first appeared in Jian'an, where most of the tea made for tribute use was produced. At that time, there were 1,336 official and private tea baking shops nestled around the Beiyuan hills, so it was only natural for a kind of competition to be created for appraising the quality of various teas from different workshops around the area. Fan Zhongyan, a famous writer and scholar of the Song described the tea competition thusly:

🍵 *Liu Songnian: Tea competition (Song Dynasty)*

"Before presenting the tribute tea to the Emperor, tea craftsmen in the Beiyuan hills

Tea competition (Sang Dynasty)

gathered to compete with each other. Baking pods scattering around, clear water from the Zhongling River boiling in cooking pots, tea dust flying in mortars, snow-white tea foam bubbling in the cups of the craftsmen, the game tea was a grand spectacle. The delicate fragrance of the tea, more pleasant than any other smell, floated in the air, greatly refreshing people's minds. When the game was set, the winner would be elated as if walking on air; the loser as ashamed as a defeated soldier."

The tea competition blazed a new trail for the art of tea as originally recorded in *The Book of Tea* by Lu Yu. Traditionally, when tea leaves were directly cooked in a pot, drinkers often sat beside to observe the changes in the tea water, meditating on the profound mysteries of nature. In the Song Dynasty, however, people usually poured boiling water into cups where tea dust was placed, and stirred the water with a bamboo brush to make the tea and water completely blend with each other, resulting in a powerful foam which grew like the head on a glass of beer. The person who could stir up the best-looking foam would win, but what really counted were the quality, appearance, and fragrance of the tea leaves, and the tea brewing skills of the competitors. In the modern Japanese tea ceremony, for example, tea is still made from tea dust, but the art of making foam is no longer practiced. In recent years, however, the tea ceremony held in Fuzhou has brought this special and ancient art to light again.

Tea cup made of celadon (Song Dynasty)

As the tea competition flourished throughout the country, tea sets, especially tea cups, were given more importance by the Song people, who were quite fond of light-colored tea, so tea accessories made of celadon, which could better set off the various colors of tea, were highly prized.

In the view of ancient Chinese literati, however, the tea competition was artificial and lacked the natural aesthetic characteristics unique to tea. The scholars paid more attention to the environment and atmosphere of the tea ceremony. For instance, Fan Zhongyan, the great philosopher, liked to recite poems and play the zither by a riverside pavilion, surrounded by rare birds and ancient trees, a pot of tea brewing by his side.

31

The famous Song poet Su Dongpo thought the natural rhythm contained in tea could only be perfected while learning how to collect water and by brewing the tea in the wild on a moonlit night, when the bell toll from an ancient temple and the call of the watch from the city wall echoed in the air.

Although the skills of tea making had made great progress in the Song Dynasty, such exotic fineries as tea cakes in the shape of dragons and phoenixes proved to be too expensive and luxurious for ordinary people, and were seemingly at odds, philosophically and aesthetically, with the simple, common elegance of tea as appealing to all social classes.

The Yuan Dynasty was established by the Mongols, a "foreign" dynasty in the sense that the Mongols were an ethnic minority and non-Han Chinese. The Mongols were originally nomadic people in the extreme north of the Chinese empire. In the early Yuan the Mongols could hardly agree to the exquisite cultural fineries of the Song, but with the established tradition of Han culture and the need to balance their diet heavy in meat and dairy products, the Mongols soon embraced tea culture and simplified it to its most basic elements. As a result, tea cakes began to fade away, and other common varieties of tea were now mass produced, such as tender tea (similar to modern green tea, whose leaves were picked in early Spring), tea dust (similar to that used in the Japanese tea ceremony), and nut tea (comprising tea with ground walnut, pine nut, sesame, apricot, and chestnut). Nut tea, for example, was welcomed among ordinary people. Even today, nut tea is still enjoyed by people in Hunan and Hubei provinces.

In the Song Dynasty tea was used in various rites by the imperial court, nobility, and the literati, while in the Yuan Dynasty tea moved even closer to appealing to ordinary people in all walks of life. Tea was representative of folk customs at the time; for instance, newly married girls showed respect for their new in-laws and guests by presenting tea. Tea was also a common subject in Song paintings, which described the tea

Yuan Dynasty art

competition among ordinary people. The anonymous painting, *Steamed Bread and Hot Tea*, vividly portrayed young brothers drinking tea and tasting steamed bread together. Such paintings reflect the affinity of tea with people's relationships. In a dynasty such as the Yuan, which drew upon many of China's ethnic minorities to fill positions within the civil administration, this affinity was especially important.

The Yuan followed their predecessors in advocating a simple and natural way of enjoying the tea ceremony. They usually made and drank tea in the hills, by rivers, under ancient trees, and in front of thatched cottages. It was a reaction against the overtly luxurious style of the Song Dynasty, and also a manifestation of the Yuan peoples' wish to remain close to nature.

The Ming Dynasty (1368-1644) was inevitably confronted with many social problems, such as the surviving forces of the Mongols, the power struggle inside the imperial court, and the numerous peasant uprisings which continually posed a threat to the dynasty's mandate of rule. The Ming rulers had to adopt a heavy-handed policy in an effort to consolidate their power, and the literati were the first to bear the brunt. Scholars were forbidden to hold gatherings, and were liable to be accused of opposing the court at every move, lest their thoughts or writings were judged to be influential to rebels. In such circumstances, many intellectuals found tea a good means to express their noble aspirations and their contempt for needless bureaucracy.

🍵 *Emperor Taizu, Ming Dynasty*

Zhu Quan, the seventeenth son of the first Ming Emperor, had helped Zhu Di, the fourth son, to usurp the throne. But unfortunately the new Emperor became suspicious of Zhu Quan and exiled him to the south. Feeling as depressed as the literati, Zhu Quan, a faithful disciple of Buddhism and Taoism, began to pursue the life of a recluse, and to also take a strong interest in the tea ceremony. Zhu Quan wrote a work entitled *A Manual on Tea,* proposing the purification of people's minds by drinking tea and advocating reforms of the ceremonial procedures established after the abolition of extravagant tea cakes. His proposals were the basis

33

which shaped the form and spirit of the Ming tea ceremony. The literati at the time usually burnt incense before the tea ceremony to air the room and worship heaven and earth; then they laid the table with tea accessories and began to boil water, grind tea leaves, and brew tea while stirring out the bubbles with a whisk. Zhu Quan himself often made his teapot in the shape of a Taoist alchemic vessel, and covered it with a rattan cover after the simple style of the ancients. Bamboo, a symbol of natural strength and moral integrity, was later used as the covering.

Many books on tea culture appeared during the Song Dynasty. For instance, Gu Yuanqing wrote a book also called *A Manual on Tea,* and Xu Xianzhong wrote *A Complete Gamut of Waters.* These books, similar to Lu Yu's *The Book of Tea,* summoned up the development of tea culture through the ages and described the new features of tea culture in the early Ming Dynasty.

 *Wen Zhengming: Tea Ceremony at Huishan (Ming Dyansty)*

Several painters also made a contribution to the promotion of tea culture. For example, *The Tea Ceremony at Huishan Hill, Lu Yu and His Tea, Tasting Tea* by Wen Zhengming, *Making Tea, Playing the Zither and Tasting Tea,* and *With Fragrant Green Tea,* vividly presented the life of leisure of the Ming literati—beside gurgling mountain springs or surging rivers, inside ancient pavilions, they played the zither and drank tea, voicing their aspirations to the green mountains and white clouds, and encouraging themselves to hold fast to their integrity amidst the political and social adversity of the period.

In the later Ming, the active part in the tea ceremony waned because of the repressive policy adopted by the imperial court toward the literati. Scholars now had to move the tea ceremony into their houses, and the natural, noble qualities were gradually lost. Many new devices were added to the tea ceremony: for instance, the "100 Tea Patterns," which referred to the ripples of various patterns which could be stirred forth in a cup of tea by means of a special brush or whisk.

Deeper involvement into ordinary people's lives was a feature of the tea culture of the Qing Dynasty (1644-1911). Like the Mongols, the Qing Dynasty was founded by the Manchus, another non-Han minority in China's northeast. The superb skills needed for the tea ceremony and the profound spirit expressed in the tea culture developed in the Ming Dynasty were too far removed from the life of ordinary people, so during the Qing some adaptations were made. The most conspicuous change was the popularity of public tea houses, where people of different social strata intermingled and communicated freely with each other. As tea was welcomed by more and more people, tea accessories consequently became simplified, leaving the teapot and cups to play the leading role. The tea set was often called the "set of Mother and Son," because it was like a mother nursing her sons when tea was poured into the cups from the pot.

Though the number of items needed for a set of tea accessories was now fewer in number, the quality and workmanship of

🌸 *Public teahouses in Beijing (Qing Dynasty)*

pots, cups, and other tea-related items grew considerably. This is especially true of the teapot. More shapes were designed, and more materials, such as purple clay, copper, porcelain, gold, silver, jade, and cloisonné enamel, were developed to improve upon the craft of tea pot making. At the time, the export of tea commenced on a large scale. Tea

🌸 *Teapot (Qing Dynasty)*

sets were sold abroad as some of the finest examples of Chinese handicrafts.

Collectors inside and outside China gradually made tea ware a status symbol, and so began in earnest the desire to collect Chinese tea pots. Moreover, whenever there were foreign guests visiting China, it was assured that they would be met and greeted with a pot of freshly brewed tea. Drinking tea as a social custom and part of the etiquette of China, spread to other parts of the world quickly, and tea culture soon became a treasure of all humanity.

Currently, there are over 50 countries that produce tea, with a annual output of 2.9 million tons.

37

🍵 *Exporting tea. Shanghai (Later Qing Dynasty)*

Chapter 3

3. Brewing and Tasting

The tea ceremony itself remains the core of Chinese tea culture and also refers to the technique and artistic process of making, brewing, and tasting tea, while also considering the spirit with which the process is undertaken. Tea and tea culture is itself visible, while its spirit is invisible. Together they form a truly unique aesthetic combination.

The art of tea also encompasses the process of planting and selecting tea as a means of artistic enjoyment. To the Chinese people, tea is like a free spirit. When tea enters the body, one is immediately filled with the nutrition of sunshine, the bright moon, the richness of the land, and the wonderment of the entire universe. Therefore, all of the famous Chinese experts on tea, have, through the centuries, shared the experience of planting, picking, and making tea themselves as a deeply personal ritual. Lu Yu traveled along the Yangtze River and Taihu Lake. He clambered up towering sheer cliffs overgrown with lush foliage. He slept in ancient Taoist temples or in the homes of tea growers in the villages scattered throughout the tea growing regions. Through such practices, he began to understand the characteristics of tea in a profound way, dedicating his life to the pursuit of tea in the process.

Mt. Wuyi (Fujian Province)

Tea trees usually grow on the northern slopes of hills with moderate rain and sunshine. Therefore, most of the growing areas of famous teas are very beautiful. Lu Yu evaluated the 31 tea-growing prefectures of the Tang Dynasty, eight of which were located in Sichuan Province. The second largest tea growing area was around Taihu Lake, with its vast expanse of misty, rolling waters, clear springs, and surrounded by beautiful mountain forests. It possessed a most suitable climate and soil for growing tea. Lu Yu built a house near the lake, and wrote *The Book of Tea* on nearby Zhushan Mountain.

Tea produced in Sichuan, Zhejiang, and Jiangxi provinces, as well as at Mt. Wuyi in Fujian Province, is still very famous even today. During the Song Dynasty, people thought highly of Jianzhou tea produced in Fujian Province, and many tea growers went deep into the mountains to look for suitable locations for growing new crops. During the Ming Dynasty, Wuyi tea was highly popular. With its cavernous and serene mountain roads and magnificent scenery, Mt. Wuyi attracted many tea growers. Some tea growers even built villas in the Bright Moon Gorge located nearby, and planted various teas there to evaluate their qualities. They studied tea from childhood to adulthood, and, after decades of learning, tasting, and trying all manner of tea-growing experiments, finally grasped the deepest, most spiritual meaning of tea.

41

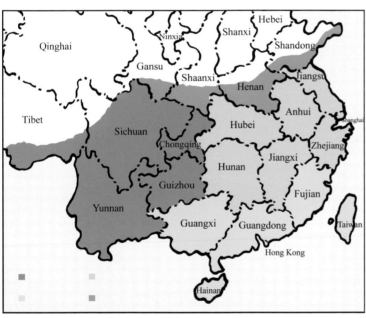

🍵 *Map of tea growing regions in China*

Zhuang Zi, one of the founders of Chinese Taoism, believed that only the things which agreed with natural laws were truly beautiful. The whole process of Chinese tea reflects this concept of the human relationship with nature.

The harvesting of tea is very important. It was not very strictly followed during the Tang Dynasty, where tea could be harvested in February, March, or April by the reckoning of the lunar calendar. During the Song Dynasty, however, the harvesting of tea became strictly regulated. The best time for harvesting was usually between the period of the Waking of Insects (one of the 24 solar terms in the Chinese calendar, beginning in early March according to the Gregorian calendar, when the weather becomes warmer, and the hibernating animals are about to come up out of the ground to move about); and the period of Pure Brightness (beginning in early April), when the temperature becomes noticeably warmer. It is best to pick tea leaves in the early hours of sunny days, when morning dew has not yet dispersed. Once the sun rises, the moisture content of tea leaves will be affected.

Tea is picked with the fingernails instead of the fingertips, so that its quality is not affected by skin temperature. The grade of the tea can be judged by the shape and tenderness of the tea buds. Generally speaking, the more tender the bud, the better the tea. A single bud looks like a lotus flower which has just come into bloom, and so is called *lianrui* (lotus bud); two buds are called *qiqiang* (tassel on a spear); three buds, which look like a small bird opening its beak, are called *queshe* (sparrow's tongue).

The process of making tea is also an artistic procedure. In the Tang Dynasty, there were four varieties of tea: weak tea, loose tea, tea dust, and tea cake. Weak tea was similar to modern brick tea, which could be stored and transported easily, but was not of high quality. Loose tea, which was similar to modern loose tea, would be collected right after being cured. Tea dust was ground into fine powder for convenient use and ease of transport. The three abovementioned varieties were used by people in their daily lives. Tea in cake form was a manifestation of the art of tea in its highest form. In the Song Dynasty, eight cakes of Great Dragon tea equaled one *jin,* which was rather heavy, while Little Dragon tea took twelve cakes to equal one *jin*, and was exquisitely shaped. Some cakes were square; some looked like six-petal plum blossoms, and some like elongated pointed jade tablets which were held in the hands of ancient rulers on ceremonial occasions. They were also decorated with various designs such as dragons, phoenixes, cloud formations, and other auspicious symbols.

The relationship between water and tea is similar to that between water and wine. Wine experts understand that excellent water quality is essential for the best grapes, while tea is even more dependent on water, not only for the preparation of the brewing of tea, but for the growth of the tea plant. It is simply impossible to make fragrant tea without good water. Therefore, famous tea experts are all knowledgeable in how they recommend the use of water.

According to Xu Cishu, a tea expert of the Ming Dynasty, tea's finest qualities can be brought into play with the help of water. Experts in the Qing Dynasty even regarded water as more important than tea itself. A truly excellent cup of tea contained only 20 percent tea but 80 percent water. If you could not taste the flavor of a fine tea, it was probably because of poor water quality.

According to Lu Yu, the water used to brew tea should be different from ordinary drinking water. Water from mountains was the best, river water was good to inferior, and well water was even worse. The water from mountain springs was better than the water taken from a waterfall. The water from mountains would become undrinkable if it stayed stagnant and still for too long a time. Tea water, therefore, should be drawn from clear flowing water in sparsely populated areas. Dew drops from mountain stalactites, clear flowing springs, and clear river streams were regarded as the sources of the best water for brewing tea.

43

Zhang Youxin, a tea expert of the Tang Dynasty, wrote *Notes on Brewing Tea* following Lu Yu's own experience. Zhang listed the following sources of water ideal for brewing tea, arranged in the order of their quality:

Spring water (Jinan, Shandong Province)

* Kangwanggu Valley, Mt. Lushan, Jiangzhou.
* Huishan Mountain Spring in Wuxi, Changzhou.
* Lanxi Mountain Spring, Qizhou.
* The frog-shaped river in the fan-shaped valley, Xiazhou.
* Huqiu Temple Spring on Tiger Hill, Suzhou.
*The pool under the Stone Bridge of the Zhaoxian Temple on Lushan Mountain, Jiangzhou.

*Lingshui Lake, Yangzhou.

*West Hills Waterfall, Hongzhou.

*Huaishui River, Tangzhou.

*Dinglong Spring on Lushan Mountain, Jiangzhou.

*Temple Well in Danyang County, Runzhou.

*Lingshui Lake in the upper reaches of the Hanjiang River.

*Chunxi Brook in the Yuxu Cave, Guizhou.

*West Valley in Wuguan, Shangzhou.

*Wusongjiang River, Suzhou.

*Southern Peak Waterfall on the Heavenly-Terrace Mountain, Zhaozhou.

*Binzhou Garden Spring.

*Yanling Beach at Tonglu, Yanzhou.

*Freshly fallen snow

Three billion people in over 160 countries drink tea on a regular basis. Tea is the most consumed drink in the world.

Emperor Qianlong of the Qing Dynasty (reigned 1736-1796) possessed a deep affection for traditional Chinese culture. The Emperor was especially keen on tea culture and held his own views on water quality as a result of his extensive travels throughout the empire, and the empirical experiments he conducted to measure the weight or density of various water sources. The Emperor would weigh the water with a special silver *dou* (or scale) whenever he found what appeared to be a particularly outstanding source of water. He concluded that water from Jade Spring Hill in Beijing's western suburbs as well as the Yixun River beyond the Great Wall was the lightest; while water from the Pearl Spring in Jinan and the Gold Hill Spring on the

Emperor Qianlong of the Qing Dynasty

Yangtze River bank ranked second and third, in terms of weight, respectively.

Tea experts in past dynasties all had a different understanding of water, and they arranged famous sources of water in different order. In truth, there is no correct answer as to which type of water is best, because the natural environment changes over time and the quality of water in the same place will not remain constant. Lu Xing, another tea expert, put forward an important principle—that tea as an art form cannot exist without water of the highest quality. Some experts, on the other hand, believed it to be unnecessary to brew tea with famous sources of water, and that water from all manner of "ordinary" sources was suitable, so long as it was taken and treated with care. For example, even water from the Yangtze River could be drawn at midnight from its upper or middle reaches, an area surrounded by rich vegetation. Others took water from the first snow, morning dew, and light drizzle. Such water, which should be caught with utensils before it falls on the ground, is referred to as "rootless water." This method of taking water, in particular, implied a linkage between tea and the universal spirit of human beings with nature. As far back as the Han Dynasty, Emperor Han Wu Di had in his possession a bronze statue of an "immortal catching the dew." Today, there is still such a bronze statue in Beihai Park in Beijing—an immortal holding a plate high to catch rain and dew from heaven. Thus, the ethos of tea and tea culture fully reflected Taoist ideologies concerning the synergistic relationship between the human world and nature.

An old Chinese idiom goes, "it is necessary to have effective tools to do good work." As a material activity, tea culture reflects the spiritual and artistic realms. Tea sets, therefore, should not only be convenient to use, but also demonstrate orderliness and an aesthetic feeling in their arrangement and operation. Lu Yu designed 24 vessels which were recorded in *The Book of Tea:*

1. Stove. Used to make a fire, it was designed in accordance with the Taoist five-element theory, and also reflected Confucian etiquette and spirit. The stoves were usually cast in iron, while later examples were made of clay and wrapped with rattan or bamboo strips.

🍵 *Tea Stove*

45

2. Bamboo basket. A square basket woven in bamboo filigree used to pick tea. Ancient tea devotees attached great importance to the actual practice of gathering tea, and usually picked, baked, and brewed tea themselves.

3. Coal breaker. The ancients used coal as a heat source to brew tea, and believed that the quality of tea would vary with the type and intensity of fire used. The coal breaker was cast in iron with six ridges and was used to break and hold individual pieces of coal when arranging them under a pot of water.

4. Fire-clip. Used to grip coal pieces and place them into a stove.

Wang Wen: Brewing Tea (detail, Ming Dynasty)

5. Boiler. Used to brew tea. The boiler has been retained in Japanese tea ceremonies up to the present. It was made of iron or stone in the Tang Dynasty.

6. Stand. Used to hold a boiler with a stove underneath. Used until the Ming and Qing dynasties, when clay stoves were wrapped with rattan or bamboo strips.

7. Paper bag. To keep tea tightly sealed so that the fragrance would not be let out.

8. Tea roller and tea dust cleaner. The tea roller was used to grind tea, while the tea dust cleaner was used to clean the tea dust off the roller. We can see the original shape of the tea roller among the tea sets unearthed in the Temple of Dharma Gate, located in Shaanxi Province. It was composed of a rectangular mill groove and a rotating central axle.

Tea roller (Temple of Dharma Gate, Shaanxi Province)

9. Tea basket. Used to sift tea.

10. *Ze.* This was a pancake-shaped soup spoon, used to measure tea.

11. Water container: To store unboiled water.

12. Filter: A device used to filter tea water, made of copper, wood, or bamboo.

13. Gourd ladle. Used to draw water. Sometimes a wooden dipper was used instead.

14. Bamboo clip. Used to stir tea water to give full vibrancy to the properties of tea during brewing.

15. Salt stand. Used to hold powdered salt crystals. In the Tang Dynasty, salt was taken as a seasoning while drinking tea.

16. Holding jar. Used to store hot water. People in the Tang Dynasty stressed three key points when brewing tea. When the water boils for the first time, put tea into the boiler to brew it directly; the second time, ladle out the foam and put the water into the holding jar; the third time, pour the boiled water from the jar into the boiler.

Salt stand (Temple of Dharma Gate, Shaanxi Province)

 47

17. Bowls: Used instead of cups, for tasting tea.

18. *Ben:* A storage container for the bowls.

19. *Zha:* Used to wash the vessels. It was similar to a pot-scouring brush.

20. Water collector: Used to store water.

21. Dreg collector: Used to gather brewed tea leaves.

22. Cloth: Used to clean the vessels.

23. Tea set stand: Used to display a tea set. It was similar to a modern tea table.

24. Big basket: Used to store all the vessels after the completion of tea drinking activities.

It is difficult for those living in contemporary society to understand the protocol involved with formal tea drinking in ancient China. These were all necessary rites and procedures used by the ancients to perform and perfect the ritual of tea preparation and drinking. A person could also change his mood

陶寶文

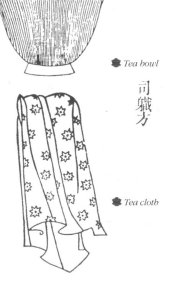

Tea bowl

司職方

Tea cloth

and temper his practical ability through the use of such vessels. People who understand Chinese cooking culture all know that the system of meticulously designing, arranging, combining, and rationally using food and drink vessels was practiced on a grand scale, as we can see from the bronze wares of the Yin, Shang, and Zhou dynasties.

In recent years, several tea sets were unearthed in the Temple of Dharma Gate in Shaanxi Province. They were given to the temple as a charitable donation by the Tang Emperor Xi Zong (873-889); and they were so exquisite, ingenious, luxurious, and splendid, that they went beyond the descriptions in Lu Yu's *The Book of Tea*. The vessels included a tea roller, basket, *ze* and salt stand, chopsticks, and bowls. Some were carved with Emperor Xi Zong's nickname: "The Fifth Brother," as well as the vessels' weight, and their manufacturer. Most of the tea sets were gilded with silver, and decorated with the Taoist patterns of an immortal riding a crane and other auspicious symbols.

🍵 *Tea box (Temple of Dharma Gate, Shaanxi Province)*

Such exquisite vessels won people's great admiration. One of them, an olive-green bowl made of "porcelain of a secret color," which was as bright as glass, is a rare and outstanding example of ancient china ware. Various beautiful colors would appear when the bowl was filled with tea.

During the Song Dynasty, tea sets were similar to those of the Tang Dynasty. However, to meet the needs of the tea competition, people paid special attention to the qualities and colors of bowls. Because those participating in the tea competition often had to try and whip up light-colored foam, special attention was paid to black and celadon ware, which would set off the natural color of tea and the tea foam to its best advantage. Special natural decorative patterns appeared on some black chinaware when it was glazed or fired in kilns.

🍵 *Black chinaware "rabbit-hair" cup (Song Dynasty)*

48

For example, the "heaven-eye" bowl, whose decorative patterns were like eyes in a black sky; and the small "rabbit-hair" cup, whose decorative patterns looked as if white hairs were growing out of the animal's black fur, are regarded as treasures among tea sets.

During the Ming Dynasty, vessels in groups were abandoned in order to simplify the sets, and attention was mainly focused on teapots and bowls. Many exquisite tea sets were produced in the Ming Dynasty, the peak period in the technical development of Chinese ceramic arts. The teapots were of high quality and crafted in novel, fanciful styles. There were many porcelain tea sets, including the ones made of ruby red and blue and white porcelain. Teapots themselves varied in style: long, flat, square, or rounded, with a loop or symmetrically arranged side handles. Most of the designs depicted flowers and birds, although figures and landscapes were also important subjects.

49

Blue porcelain teapot with handle (Ming Dynasty)

Tea sets were made of other materials other than traditional china or porcelain, such as *zisha* ware. The brilliant achievements of Chinese pottery and porcelain occupied an important place at the dawn of the history and the emerging culture of food. Later, bronze and iron ware appeared, and pottery was relegated to a lesser position, although porcelain china continued to be used because of its fine, delicate qualities. To meet the needs of the emerging tea culture, the status of what was once considered ancient pottery was greatly raised to a new level.

During the Ming Dynasty, tea sets and all the various tea making paraphernalia were slowly abandoned, and people took to brewing tea in teapots directly. Porcelain teapots were so impermeable that the tea would spoil if kept too long in them. The *zisha* pottery pot was invented to solve this problem. It was made of special clay from Yixing, Xianyang, Chaozhou, and other nearby cities. In the Ming Dynasty, a single *zisha* teapot could sometimes equal the entire wealth of an average family. People were so fond of exquisite *zisha* teapots that they tried desperately to attain or even collect them, in some cases, sending themselves down the road to financial ruin in the process.

Zisha pottery pot made by Chen Manshen (Qing Dynasty)

This phenomenon continued until the Qing Dynasty. *Zisha* teapots have always been treasured by collectors. Today there is a thriving industry which offers genuine *zisha* pottery to tea lovers all over the world at a reasonable price.

Because pottery clay absorbs fragrances easily, an excellent *zisha* teapot is full of the tea's essence after it has been used for a long time, and will send forth a refreshing fragrance immediately whenever people use it. The Chinese people always advocate simplicity and naturalness, and the *zisha* teapots are outstanding examples of these characteristics. The *zisha* teapot is also treasured because of the artistic designs of the craftsmen who created them.

The first *zisha* teapot was supposedly invented by an anonymous monk of the Golden Sand Temple. However, for all practical purposes, its real originator was Gong Chun, and the teapot invented by him was simply called the Gong Chun Teapot. Gong Chun was a servant boy in a scholar's studio. He was greatly influenced by Buddhism because he lived in the Golden Sand Temple at the time he tried to make the teapot. The formation of his unique artistic style may be attributed to many factors. His works were very simple and elegant in color and shape, and were lively and diverse in style: some looked like red melons full of the fragrance of earth; some were

Gong Chun Teapot

like tree stumps, which looked like old men telling the long history of tea; some were like fragrant buds, which naturally suited the essence of tea.

Shi Dabin, an expert succeeding Gong Chun, often visited the Songjiang River. He had close contact with Chen Jiru, a famous tea expert of the Ming Dynasty, and absorbed Chen's ideas on tea culture. The design of Shi's work was ingeniously conceived. For example, a small teapot looked like a monk's cap, which naturally reminded one of a monk praying to Buddha in an ancient temple. The message was clear: you drink tea to purify your soul, and the teapot would bring you immediately into the Buddha's realm.

Monk's cap Teapot by Shi Dabin (Ming Dynasty)

The methods of drinking tea have changed several times since the Han and Tang dynasties. Tea dust is brewed directly in teapots. This method was most popular before the Tang Dynasty. Lu Yu introduces the whole process in detail in *The Book of Tea*. First, tea cakes are ground into dust with a tea roller, and then choice water is poured into a teapot. Brew it over a fire on a stove heated by coal, and add the tea dust when the water has come to a rolling boil. The tea and water would blend with each other. Foam appears when the water boils for a second time; the foam is called *bomo*. Lu Yu regarded this as the so-called "cream" of tea, which should be ladled out and kept in a jar. Tea and water further blend together, and waves appear when the water boils for the third time; *bomo* is then returned to the teapot. The resulting liquid is called *Jiufei* or *Yuhua*. When the cream becomes evenly blended, the tea is ready to be served.

51

A method known as the drip tea method came into being in the Tang Dynasty, and became popular in the Song Dynasty, when people did not brew tea in teapots. Tea cakes are ground into powder, and then placed in tea bowls with gently-boiled water poured over them. The tea and water will blend, so special attention should be paid to the

Anonymous: Serving Tea (Fresco on the wall of a tomb, Liao Dynasty)

teapot brush, the utensil used for stirring tea. Most of the brushes used are made of bamboo. The quality and quantity of foam is determined by brush shape and one's stirring skill. Pour the water into a tea bowl, and strike the bowl hard with the brush. Tea and water will blend, and *bomo* would gradually appear, looking like white clouds or snow. The quality of tea should be judged by whether foam appears soon and water waves appear late. A tea with white foam, and its water waves appearing late without dispersing, is regarded as tea of the highest grade, and tea connoisseurs will notice this immediately. It has been recorded that the tea foam stirred by a tea devotee of the Song Dynasty looked like white clouds or snow piling above the bowl. In recent years, tea enthusiasts have been studying this method, and they can also make foam rise above the rim of the bowl, but the foam does not resemble clouds, and remains concave in the middle. This might be due to the shape of the teapot brush and the method used to stir tea, which are different from those methods used in centuries past. The present-day Japanese tea ceremony still uses the bamboo brush to stir the tea, however, the tea dust is finely ground and the stirring force is usually not strong enough to produce foam resembling a cloud.

52

A method known as "Dripping Flower Tea" was created by Zhu Quan during the Ming Dynasty. The tea made in this way possessed a special fragrance and contributed a unique artistic effect. Put the buds of plum blossoms, sweet-scented osmanthus, and jasmine, together with tea dust into a bowl, and speed the opening of the buds with steam. You may then enjoy its color, fragrance, and taste simultaneously, as it is also a feast for the eyes as well as the nose and mouth.

Another method is known as "Semi-Made Tea." Add walnuts, melon seeds, pine nuts, and other dry fruits to the tea, and pour in boiling hot water. Tea enthusiasts used to enjoy themselves by picking, brewing, and drinking semi-made tea in high mountains and on open plains.

One of the most common processes is known as "Made Tea,"

🍵 *Green Tea*

and has been used since the Ming and Qing dynasties. Although it is simple and convenient, great differences exist between various geographic regions and varieties of tea used. It requires a different length of time to make red tea (what is typically known as black tea in the West), green tea, and scented (or herbal) tea. The optimum water temperature for brewing also varies with they type of tea. Green tea is particularly delicate, so the water temperature should not be excessively high. For example, Longjing (Dragon Well) tea would become tasteless after pouring hot water on it two or three times. Red tea is hard, and the blades are thick, so it takes a longer time to brew correctly. Scented tea requires moderate temperature and brewing time.

 *Wu Changsuo: Tasting Tea (Qing Dynasty)*

True tea connoisseurs would not merely make tea just to drink; they would first appreciate the shape of the tea, analyzing its variety as well as any aspects of its physical characteristics or smell. Various teas have different shapes both when dry and when wet. Their appearance in the water can often be markedly different from their appearance when dry.

Made tea requires one to pour skillfully. Tea makers with excellent skills can go the rounds, pouring the tea evenly from a teapot into a dozen cups on a plate without spilling a drop.

Thus, tea is truly a performance art, requiring a special environment and state-of-mind. In ancient times there were many participants in large tea parties and imperial tea feasts. For example, Emperors Kangxi and Qianlong of the Qing Dynasty held top-grade tea feasts in the Hall of Supreme Harmony in the Forbidden City, with thousands of participants at each such feast. However, according to the theory of the traditional Chinese tea ceremony, it is unnecessary to have so many participants. Traditional tea drinking simply required one to drink tea

54

in a simple, aesthetically pleasing environment, such as by a clear spring or in a bamboo groves high on a mountain; in ancient temples and small pavilions, or in one's own garden while appreciating the beauty of nature. Such elaborate and ornate feasts represented the opposite of what tea drinking meant to so many scholars, artists, and philosophers through the centuries, who much preferred a simpler approach. Many artists of the Ming Dynasty painted such seemingly idyllic environments. For example, the painting *Tasting Tea* by Tang Yin depicts tea devotees drinking tea in a bright hay-thatched hall surrounded by ancient trees and a growth of green plants under bamboo fences on a lofty green mountain. In the Ming Dynasty, most tea enthusiasts built teahouses in their own courtyards and villas. There they would burn incense to purify the air, and wash all the tea sets before drinking, and then invite friends to drink tea while writing poems, painting, or having long, flowing discussions under the moonlight.

55

Tang Yin: Tasting Tea (Ming Dynasty)

Chapter 4

4. Tea in Philosophy and Religion

Those who have watched the traditional Japanese tea ceremony often ask: why is it called a formal tea "ceremony" in Japan and simply a kind of tea "art" in China? Is it because China has no tea ceremony, or that the Chinese ceremony is somehow not as traditional as the Japanese tea ceremony?

In fact, China was the birthplace of the tea ceremony before it migrated to Japanese society. The question will arise because of an overall lack of knowledge about the history and development of tea culture in China and Japan, but also because of the different understanding of the meaning of the term *Dao* in Chinese and Japanese civilization. According to the Chinese, for example, *Dao,* or "the Way," is the essential nature, origin, and law of a thing. This way of nature is invisible, and is perceived rather than seen. Consequently, the Chinese rarely associate *Dao* to anything so readily. In Japanese, *Dao* refers to "skills." As a cultural activity, tea ceremony is assigned the title of *Dao* as well. The Chinese people believe that the artistic process of drinking tea is merely a form, which tends to be flawed and superficial, while the true intent is to best express one's inner spirit. The Chinese and Japanese also regard tea art and the tea ceremony as different aspects of the same puzzle. Tea art is a visible material activity, but only if the personal, spiritual force is aroused at some point during the activity can it be truly called *Dao* to the Chinese mind. The core of tea culture is thus the "visible art and invisible *Dao.*" In fact, Lu Yu, together with other leading experts of tea in past dynasties, manifested the shared spirit through the continual development of tea culture.

🍵 *Dao, or " The Way"*

The spirit of the Chinese tea ceremony is a broad and profound system absorbing many essential elements of Confucian, Taoist, and Buddhist thought. This synthesis fully illustrates the Chinese traditional idea of the close integration and interaction between the material and the spiritual world.

Each civilization has its own unique cultural system and individual social characteristics. Historically, great differences have existed in the orientation of culture and values between East and West. The West advocates the use of fire and preservation of power, while China is characterized as peaceful, gentle and kind, firm yet tenacious. Tea, which is also gentle and peaceful, has been influenced by philosophy and religion in accordance with these characteristics. Though Taoism and Buddhism have played important roles in the development of tea culture, Confucian thought is regarded as the core of the spirit of the Chinese tea ceremony.

It has often been said that Western civilization is open and enthusiastic. The culture of wine is synonymous with the West. The cultures of the East, such as China and Japan, possess a disposition resembling tea: sober, sensible, gentle, and enduring. Similarly, Chinese culture emphasizes the development of human relations in a collective—as opposed to strictly individual—manner. This is a key Confucian concept which was introduced into the tea ceremony, advocating the creation of a harmonious atmosphere through the drinking of tea. In ancient times, foreign envoys were served tea at the imperial court, while even today, tea is offered in formal and informal settings as a way to express friendliness and sincerity, as well as to strengthen solidarity. Such rituals extend to nearly every area of Chinese culture.

Tea culture is a paradox in itself. Although water and fire seem incompatible from a purely elemental point of view, Lu Yu stressed their interdependence. How could one boil water without fire? And how could a person make tea without water? Therefore, Lu Yu molded the images of firebirds, fish, and waves on tea pots, in order to show the relationship between wind, fire, and water. The spirit of solidarity and harmony is carried out in each link of tea culture. The painting entitled *100 Children* by Su Hanchen, which, as its title suggests, depicts 100 children drinking tea while playing, paints an idyllic picture of a society living in complete harmony. In the Qing Dynasty, an artist named Chen Mingyuan crafted a teapot whose body was made of tightly-bound roots of three old trees. The teapot shared three roots,

Roots in the form of Cha (Tea)

a pot of water, and a lid, expressing the old proverb of "unity is strength" and that it is impossible, for example, to break 10 pairs of chopsticks simultaneously. This teapot also expressed the idea that despite their differing folk customs, all ethnic groups of China were linked together by their common "roots."

The Chinese believe in a pantheon of gods and immortals, many of whom were human at one time but through acts of extreme self sacrifice, became ethereal beings revered by society. Within this belief is the perception of the self-perpetuating strength of humankind. Therefore, in the Chinese tea ceremony, imperial concubines and princesses in the imperial palace could drink tea while appreciating music; scholars would drink tea while listening to music, writing calligraphy, reciting poems, or contemplating the peace, serenity, and harmony of their surroundings.

Even monks gained enlightenment and inner peace by drinking tea. Jiao Ran, a notable monk of the Tang Dynasty, and a friend of Lu Yu, helped to further enrich tea culture with Lu Yu as well as other scholars. Instead of advocating strict ascetic practices, Jiao Ran advocated the drinking of tea while appreciating fragrant flowers, the bright moon, and beautiful music, all of which were replete with strong emotional and spiritual meaning. Jiao Ran was an accomplished poet, and often composed poems inspired by tea drinking.

The Chinese view the characteristic of bitterness as a means of tempering the human soul. The idea is that bitterness will not last very long, due to the fact that nature is always in motion. Tea is consumed to allow development of the human spirit, and the desire to help others and exhibit generosity.

Some people have misunderstood the pastime of tea drinking as merely an idle pastime for hermits and the like. During the Ming and Qing dynasties, many tea connoisseurs were, in fact, social pessimists. At the end of the Qing Dynasty, the Manchus of the "Eight Banners" (the military-administrative organizations of the Manchus in the Qing Dynasty) regarded tea as nothing more than a plaything, with no redeeming social value. However, when one considers that the Confucian spirit has been the main element of tea culture for hundreds of years; Chinese intellectuals have shown a strong sense of social responsibility, always voicing their concern and compassion for society and the affairs of the common people.

As far back as the Eastern and Western Jin, and the Southern dynasties period, Lu Na, Huan Wen, and several other politicians helped to create and perpetuate early tea culture and its role in society, advocating the cultivation of morality and honesty. Tea was seen as a way to attain a higher social and moral plateau in Chinese society. Lu Yu formally created the system of Chinese tea culture in the Tang Dynasty, synthesizing Confucian, Taoist and Buddhist thought, with the Confucian attitude towards life as the guiding principle.

Lu Yu was concerned about his country and his people. An internal rebellion led by An Lushan, had just been put down when Lu Yu began to make tea stoves. Lu Yu was taking refuge in Huzhou City and the good tidings that the country had become stable again filled him with joy. The boiler made by Lu Yu had a square handle, symbolizing honesty; wide edges, which symbolized lofty ideals; and a long base, which symbolized the Golden Mean of Confucianism.

Most of the tea connoisseurs maintained the fine tradition of acquiring and using specific tea sets. In the middle and later periods of the Ming Dynasty, most of the Emperors were fatuous and self-indulgent; the tea connoisseurs therefore paid special attention to cultivating integrity by not associating themselves with undesirable elements. They wrapped stoves with bamboo and called them *kujiejun* (following the characteristic unique to bamboo, which refers to preserving moral integrity amid adversity). This suggested that the tea connoisseurs endeavored to learn from the natural form, physical tenacity, and aesthetic purity of bamboo.

🍵 *Tea stove cover with bamboo, or, Kujiejun*

The device used for measuring tea was the *zhiquan*.

Tea and Chinese Culture

Quan was a part of an ancient weighing apparatus—the sliding weight of a steelyard (which symbolizes the judgment of just and unjust criteria). One small tea set showed the standard of measuring, indicating that true connoisseurs could distinguish truth from falsehood.

Though its history has often been tumultuous, China is nevertheless known as a land of propriety and righteousness. Confucian philosophy regulated proper behavior and established social order. In addition, this code of social ethics implied mutual respect.

Tea was first served during Confucian ceremonies in the Song Dynasty. At that time, the tea ceremony was used on the occasion of the grand feasts held by the court in spring and autumn. The details were recorded in the *History of the Song Dynasty.* Tea would be "granted" when imperial civil service examinations were held, when the Emperor interviewed officials and received foreign envoys, and on the occasion of memorial ceremonies or various festivals. China's ethnic minorities were also affected by the system. For example, the rival State of Liao and the Song imperial court confronted each other and fought many battles. Peace was finally attained, however, and by mutual agreement they sent envoys to each other. A tea ceremony was held when the Song imperial court received the envoy from the State of Liao. Though the State of Liao was founded by nomadic people not of the Han nationality, they nevertheless appreciated the rite system of the Song Dynasty and eagerly accepted the tea as means of truce.

According to the *History of the Song Dynasty,* when a prince took an imperial concubine, he had to offer her 100 *jin* of tea together with other presents. Later, it became customary to hold tea ceremonies at weddings.

If the social influence of Chinese tea culture is mainly reflected in Confucian thought, its aesthetic attributes, skills, and practical spirit are mainly influenced by Taoist thought.

The Taoist School and Taoism are entirely different. The Taoist School in fact appeared much earlier than Confucian thought. The spirit of Confucian thought focused on administering society, while Taoist thought emphasized the relationship between man and nature. Lao Zi, the founder of Taoist thought, was born in the State of Chu more than 2,700 years ago. Lao Zi advocated looking at things dialectically, and stressed that people should see the reverse as well as the obverse side of things. For example, when others said firmness was better than softness, he would retort that one's teeth were firm, but they would drop out before he died; while the tongue was soft, it would stick with him throughout his life. When others said that bountiful qualities were good, Lao Zi would retort that only empty rooms could hold things, and one had to empty old thoughts out of one's mind before acquiring new knowledge.

🫖 *Tao De Jing (Lao Zi)*

63

Zhuang Zi, another Taoist thinker, liked to illustrate such truths through vivid fables and allegorical tales, often using humorous language. Lao Zi and Zhuang Zi both believed that it was the common law of the universe that kept nature and society operating in harmony. Therefore, spiritual and material elements, together with human law and the laws of nature, could not be separated.

🫖 *Zhuang Zi*

According to the Taoist School, the human world and the natural world are one. A single person represents the world in microcosm, while a cup of tea reflects the sea. The tea ceremony has assimilated this thought. Tea follows nature's law, and through tea we can gain a better understanding of the relationship between humanity and nature. Lu Yu regarded the process of making, brewing, and drinking tea as an intimate art reflecting natural beauty. When the ancients brewed tea, they ground tea cakes or the freshly-picked and baked tea first, then sifted it through a fine sieve, and placed the most evenly-shaped, tender powder into a boiler. The tea would undergo a miraculous change as the boiling water and fresh tea were blended together. People could appreciate natural beauty through observing such a change. Lu Yu vividly described the tea dust which was just put into the boiler as "floating date flowers in a pond," or as "the newly-grown green duckweed on a winding pond."

Lu Yu also described the foam—known as the cream of tea— vividly: it was "as white as fresh snow." Tea connoisseurs regarded tea as the cleanest and most beautiful thing in nature, so people would naturally integrate themselves with their natural setting whenever possible while drinking tea.

Lu Tong, a poet in the Tang Dynasty, felt as if misty rain and cool breezes were spraying on him, while the whole world was incomparably bright and clear whenever he drank tea. When he drank seven cups of tea, he felt as graceful as an invisible spirit. Su Shi, a great writer of the Song Dynasty, liked to row a small boat, draw water from the middle of a river, and brew tea in the rural outskirts of a town, or by the river bank. He believed that by doing so, he invited the bright moon and its silver flame into his water jar. Chinese tea connoisseurs believed that people should not merely take from nature; they should also care for it and understand its processes, and treat nature with kindness for the purpose of living in happiness and harmony. There is much that is profound about a cup of tea.

According to Taoist beliefs, tea could contribute to good health and a long life. The main underlying precept of Taoism was to discard all desires and worries from one's mind; the best method of preserving one's health was by keeping one's body and mind extremely peaceful whenever possible. There were several ways to cultivate one's vital energy to reach the ideal state:

1. Using deep breaths to regulate one's air passages through which vital energy is circulated.

2. Keeping one's thoughts attuned to the rhythms of nature.

3. Imagining the brilliance of sunshine and rain washing one clean, and ridding the body of impurities.

4. Eating healthy food.

Because tea fit into this ethic perfectly, it became an essential component of Taoism. Zhu Quan, a noted expert of tea culture who lived during the Ming Dynasty, often drank tea while eating fruits and pine nuts when he meditated in the mountains. The Taoist view of the body was consistent with the teachings of traditional Chinese medicine, which advocated adjusting one's mind and physiological functions, through which the drinking of tea could aid greatly.

Taoists possessed an active outlook when it came to nature, and above all strived for coexistence between heaven and earth. Taoism followed the laws of nature. Tea connoisseurs reflected Taoist thought in the tea ceremony, thereby providing a means with which to escape depression. Most disciplined themselves by following ascetic practices to preserve their moral integrity, and so the tea set was also called *kujiejun* in the Yuan and Ming dynasties, to express their lofty ideals.

Lao Zi and Zhuang Zi, founders of the Taoist School, often spoke or acted contrary to common views intentionally. According to Lao Zi, people in the world could never find contentment in seeking pleasure; only Lao Zi was indifferent to pleasure, for he had realized the hidden danger behind high positions and great wealth. Zhuang Zi expressed his views, which were also out of keeping with common thought, even more vividly and clearly. According to Zhuang Zi, wise men were admired because there were too many confused people in the world; if everyone became wise, there would be no wise men.

Chinese tea connoisseurs tried to learn and absorb much of the characteristics of Lao Zi and Zhuang Zi. For example, despite its low social status, Lu Yu chose to become an actor; he refused to take a post in the court, and instead devoted himself to the study of tea culture. Another connoisseur of the Ming Dynasty, Zhu Quan,

🍵 *Lao Zi*

65

who was a member of the imperial family, built a tomb for himself in a remote mountain in southern China when he was still young, so that he could devote himself to the study of the Taoist and Buddhist schools. It seemed that to the true tea connoisseur, even beggars were better than corrupt officials. Thus, Taoist tea culture was more suited to scholars and common people than the literati and officialdom. As a practice and an art form the tea ceremony was natural and unrestrained.

When talking about Chinese tea culture, attention is often paid to its relationship with

Chan, or Zen

Buddhism. There is a saying both in China and Japan that "Tea and Chan (Zen) is an integration." Although Chan is only a Buddhist sect, it has made a great contribution to the formation of the spirit of the tea ceremony, and has played an important role in spreading tea culture throughout the world. The first disseminator of Japanese Buddhism was also the first tea master and the founder of the Japanese tea ceremony. The unique characteristics of the Chinese Buddhist tea ceremony aroused great attention among Japanese monks.

Tea culture was closely tied to earthly reality and society, while Buddhism stressed ultimate enlightenment and paradise. Chinese tea culture mainly stressed the love of life and optimism, while Buddhism emphasized the importance of suffering as a means to attain enlightenment. The Chan sect (known as Zen in Japan), solved this contradiction, and as a result, the two approaches were integrated.

Historically, China has resembled a large smelting furnace, in which foreign thoughts and ideas needed to be melted in or blended with the rest of the culture before they were able to grow on their own. In spite of this, the policy towards foreign cultures was open and magnanimous, especially during the Tang Dynasty, when the tea culture was created. It was during the Tang Dynasty that Buddhism was integrated into tea culture.

The majority of Buddhist sects that spread to China belonged to what was known as the "Greater Vehicle," commonly referred to as Mahayana Buddhism, which developed between the first and second century A.D. Mahayana Buddhism held that all living creatures could become Buddha, and that equal emphasis should be placed on how to benefit one's self as well as others while practicing Buddhism. Buddhists regarded such doctrines as the best and most appealing to the greatest number of people, hence the name. The sects advocating moksha (ultimate release from the cycle of rebirth), were known as the "Lesser Vehicle," or Hinayana sect. For example, the Sanlun, Sukhavati, Vinaya, and Faxiang sects were all Mahayana sects which spread to China from India. However, these religious doctrines were not to the liking of the Chinese people. For examp1e, according to the Sanlun sect, people should not be afraid of death, and should weep for life. However, Chinese society could not accept such rigid attitudes that happiness awaits one only in death.

It was clear that during the Tang Dynasty, Buddhist reform had to be carried out so Buddhist theories could be integrated with Chinese culture. Thus, the Tiantai, Huayan, and other sects, which were similar to Chinese culture and ideologies, came into being.

It was the Chan sect that came to evolve into a true Chinese Buddhist practice. Chan Buddhism advocated meditation in order to become peaceful in one's mind. It was similar to the Taoist practice of sitting in meditation, as well as the Confucian views governing one's inner accomplishment. Meditation was beneficial to one's health, and enabled purification of the mind to improve both the body and the spirit.

Hui Neng (638-713), the sixth patriarch of the Chan sect during the Tang Dynasty, advocated practicing Buddhism whenever possible, by observing that "the butcher who lays down his cleaver at once becomes a Buddha." According to Hui Neng, people could become Buddhists without becoming monks or nuns.

With the appearance of the Chan sect, Buddhism started to possess Chinese characteristics, and became consistent with existing tea culture. The Chan sect made contributions to promoting tea culture in the following three ways:

1. Popularizing the practice of drinking tea: According to the historical work, *Records of What Feng Saw and Heard*, written by Feng Yan during the Tang Dynasty, southerners liked drinking tea,

Hui Neng

while northerners did not often drink tea at first. In the middle years of the Kaiyuan reign, the master of taming demons in the Divine Rock Temple on the Taishan Mountain developed the Chan sect energetically. The monks were neither allowed to sleep nor have supper while sitting in meditation at night, but they were allowed to drink tea. So each of them brewed tea and drank it. People followed their example and tea-drinking thus became a custom. Many tea shops were opened in the city, from which everyone could buy tea. Tea produced on the mountain was great in variety and quantity, and was transported by boat and carriage from the Yangtze and Huai River valleys.

2. Developing tea plantations and planting tea on mountains: It was expensive for monasteries to buy tea for monks, so the monks in some areas started to develop tea plantations or planted their own tea crop high in the mountains. Most of the monasteries were built in remote locations to begin with, with excellent sources of clear water, rich soil, and clean air, all of which were beneficial to tea growing. Many varieties of famous teas were produced by monasteries during the Tang Dynasty. The monks on Mount Putuo planted many tea trees, and "Putuo Buddhist tea" became known throughout the empire. The tradition of the tea plantation was retained until the Ming Dynasty. Many monasteries were built in Jian'an in the Southern Tang Dynasty, and most of them planted excellent tea because both monks and pilgrims drank tea and monasteries possessed land. In addition, the monks had enough time to study the skills of planting, growing, harvesting, brewing, and tasting tea. As a result, they promoted the development of tea culture to the larger population, and Jian'an became a well-known area of tea production during the Song Dynasty.

3. Treating tea with a meditative mind, and creating the Buddhist characteristics of the tea ceremony: According to its philosophical views, the Chan sect stressed the tempering and remolding of one's disposition to find one's true self. When a person's spirit reached a morally pure state, that person would attain enlightenment. Tea would aid in the process to keep one's mind and spirit calm, clear minded, and focused during meditation. The monks of the Chan sect drank tea not only to refresh themselves; they also connected the realm of tea with that of the Chan sect, and appreciated the true essence of the world was to seek peace of mind.

Fo Tuchen, a great monk of the Western Jin Dynasty.

A key element of Buddhism is in the eradication of suffering through the elimination of desire. According to the Chan sect, it was impossible for people to eliminate all of their worries intentionally. They first had to tranquilize their hearts to grasp the spirit of the tea ceremony, which

68

was to study the relationship between tea, mountains, rivers, nature, heaven, earth, and man. By doing so, the relationship between body and mind, as well as the material and spiritual, could be understood.

In Tibet, tea culture flourished in mountain monasteries. Tibetans regarded tea as the wonder of enshrining and worshiping the Buddha. Monasteries granted tea to common people as the blessing of Buddha. At the Jokhang Temple in Lhasa, brick tea over 100 years old is still kept as a religious and cultural relic. The monks there do not drink it, but instead regard it as a symbol of blessing and a protective shield over the monastery.

According to the description of a missionary of the Qing Dynasty, over 4,000 lamas attended a gathering at the Karwenpalmo Lamasery, where ordinary believers lay on the ground to worship Buddha, young monks held hot boilers and gave tea to the people, and people started to chant phrases of praise. Because the tea was served as part of a Buddhist rite, tea became imbued with mystery. Buddha was said to save all beings, so huge vats of boiling water had to be used for such large gatherings so that enough tea could be given to the people.

The tea parties held by the Chan monasteries accentuated the adjustment of one's mind with tea to give full scope to one's ability to find one's true self, while the tea parties held by Tibetan monasteries regarded tea as a wonder granted by paradise. This view was more characteristic of objective idealism, and entirely different from the spirit of the tea ceremony of the Chan sect.

The spirit of the Chinese tea ceremony, influenced by Confucian, Taoist, and Buddhist philosophies, has come to be integrated into a unique

🍵 *Tibetan teapot*

cultural and philosophical synergy. The tea ceremony has won support among people in all walks of life. In the late Qing Dynasty and the early Republican, when China experienced from dynastic decline, revolution, and warlordism, scholars often put a brush pot, books, and a simple tea set on their tables to express and maintain their aesthetic ideals. The common people often placed a tea set on a square table in the central room of their house, and the whole family would drink tea together each night.

Chapter 5

5. Teahouse Culture

Teahouses, those public places in cities and towns where people gathered to drink tea, took shape during the Tang Dynasty and flourished during the Song Dynasty. They were popular in South China, for southerners loved drinking tea, and they could also be found everywhere in North China. There were various types of teahouses. Many varieties of tea were served in teahouses, including ordinary tea, ginger tea with seasoning, peppermint tea, and plum tea. In terms of their social function, the teahouses of the Tang and Song dynasties, however, only acted as meeting places for townspeople.

Considerable progress was made in the colorful teahouse culture from the Ming and Qing dynasties, when teahouse culture was integrated with regional culture and left an unmistakable imprint on Chinese society.

Ba-Shu is one of China's earliest famous tea producing areas. The local people have kept up the hobby of drinking tea until the present day. A familiar proverb goes, "there are few clear days, but many teahouses." In Sichuan Province, the city of Chengdu was most noted for its teahouses of various sizes. The largest of these could seat hundreds, while the smaller shops offered a more intimate setting. Sichuan teahouses stressed good service, elegant style, and above all, excellent tea, tea sets, and, of course, atmosphere—a special environment conducive to both tea drinking and socializing. Traditional Sichuan teahouses served customers with red copper teapots, tin saucers, teacups with covers made of Jingdezhen porcelain, *tuocha*—bowl-shaped compressed tea leaves— and tearoom keepers expert in all aspects of tea. Sichuan teahouses not only attracted people's attention with their great numbers and excellent service, but also with their social functions.

🍵 *Shunxing Old Teahouse (Chengdu, Sichuan Province)*

🍂 *Sichuan Teahouse*

Sichuan Province is rich in natural resources, and its local culture flourished in ancient times. During the Three Kingdoms Period, Zhuge Liang helped Liu Bei establish the State of Shu in Sichuan, which played an important role in the development of Ba-Shu culture, and Sichuanese preserved the tradition of concerning themselves with state affairs. Because of its location, access into Sichuan was often difficult, and it was hard for local people to get information about the goings on in various parts of the country. The Sichuan teahouses played an important role in spreading such information. The local people went to teahouses not only to drink tea, but also to exchange information. The most important function of the teahouses was that people could chat with each other there. Each large teahouse reflected the society in

Sichuan Teahouse

microcosm. Teahouses could be found everywhere in Chongqing, Chengdu, and other large and small cities and towns throughout Sichuan Province. In the old days, many Chongqing people liked to linger in teahouses. They would go there immediately after they woke up, and some of them even washed their faces there to refresh themselves before settling down with a pot of tea. They would drink tea and have breakfast, and then chat with each other.

Though simply furnished, Sichuan teahouses were elegant yet informal, making people feel immediately at home. Customers could sit at tables or lie on bamboo deck chairs while drinking tea. Whenever a customer entered a teahouse, and sat in a chair, the waiter would greet him warmly, and make tea for him. The tearoom keeper would take off the cover of the teacup with his left hand, while making tea with the right hand. His two hands worked in unison, and dozens of cups would be filled with tea in an instant without a single drop being spilled. The maneuver reflected the tradition of "even cream" in tea culture, and also demonstrated beautiful rhythm and superb skill. Such as sight was a visual delight for the teahouse guests.

Sichuanese enjoyed drinking *tuocha,* the bowl-shaped compressed mass of tea leaves with a strong taste and delicate fragrance, especially when they talked for a long time, as the qualities of *tuocha* were very long-lasting. Some people would drink from early morning until noon, and ask the tearoom keeper to keep their teacups at the ready so that they could continue to drink after lunch. Quick-witted, and skilled in all manner of conversation and debates, the Sichuanese could talk with old friends or make new ones with equal aplomb.

Chongqing Tuocha

Teahouses also served as unofficial courts of law. Local people would gather at a teahouse, and ask the powerful security group heads, rural elites or the *Paoge* Master (a secret society in the provinces in the southwest part of China in the old days) to settle a dispute. God knew

74

whether the resolution was fair or not. However, the practice showed that Sichuanese regarded teahouses as fair and legitimate places to settle disputes. Compared with teahouses elsewhere, Sichuan teahouses had more obvious political and social roles.

It was not true that Sichuan teahouses were vulgar and attracted the lower strata of society. In fact, many scholars often went there. It is said that some Sichuan authors liked to write in teahouses, for there they could "keep quiet in a noisy neighborhood," and draw their inspiration from the energy of the teahouses. On fair days, the seats of a local teahouse would be placed outside so that people could appreciate Sichuan opera, *qingyin* (a type of ballad-singing popular in Sichuan Province), *shuochang* (a genre of popular entertainment mainly including talking and singing), and traditional puppet shows. The teahouses served as public places for holding folk and cultural activities.

Sichuan teahouses also served as centers where business transactions were completed. Special teahouses for businessmen in Chengdu featured comfortable seats, where tea was served with light refreshments, and people could order dishes at any time. Such environments were very convenient for conducting business.

With their political, economic and cultural functions, Sichuan teahouses played an important role in society. Though they were not necessarily learned and refined places, the cultural and social functions associated with tea were fully reflected within the atmosphere of the teahouses.

🍵 *Teahouses played an important role in Chinese society*

Tea and Chinese Culture

Situated in a remote area far from the national political center, the lower Yangtze River valley retained the cultural features that formed the unique style and characteristics of the ancient culture of the states of Wu and Yue (hereafter referred to as Wu-Yue Culture). The area was long inhabited by the ancient tribes in the east. It is one of China's famous tea-producing areas and the birthplace of Chinese tea culture, for green tea produced in Zhejiang Province played a major role in the history of tea. Several important factors contributed to the region's significance to Chinese tea culture.

Noted for its beautiful landscapes, the lower Yangtze River valley not only has suitable natural conditions for producing tea, but also possesses the aesthetic environment for tasting tea. It is

🍵 *Teahouse built beside a bridge*

rich in natural features known throughout China. The Wu-Yue Area, including Taihu Lake and the neighboring river valleys, became in essence, China's greatest natural "teahouse."

Southeastern China is center of Buddhist and Taoist activity, and people there respect ancient customs and local traditions. Buddhism has kept fewer of its original features in the area than in Qinghai, Tibet, and other western regions. Any cultural characteristics have to be remolded to some degree to suit local customs. In the Wu-Yue area, Chan Buddhism is practiced. It is a completely remolded Buddhist school which is closer to Taoist and Confucian thought—China's "original" spiritual and philosophical culture.

🍵 *Feng Zikai: Teahouse of Stone-gate Bay, Tong Xiang, Zhejiang Province*

Therefore, the famous Wu-Yue tea producing region integrates Confucian, Taoist and Buddhist thought, a combination which created the systematic development of Chinese tea culture.

The economy of the lower Yangtze River valley has flourished since the Sui and Tang dynasties. The Southern Song government established its capital in Lin' an, and as a result, the local culture developed rapidly. The area is greatly affected by the fresh cultural flavor of regions south of the Yangtze, and the local culture is also blended with ancient customs. The ancient Chinese tea culture has changed dramatically in modern times, but its essence has been retained secretly not only in the Wu-Yue area, but also in Fujian and Guangdong provinces. Up to now tea markets in Zhejiang Province have been the most flourishing, and various organizations have been established. These include the Lu Yu and Jiao Ran tea groups; folk tea parties in Huzhou City; the modernized China Tea Research Institute; the tea museum in Hangzhou and the teahouses by the West Lake.

Hangzhou teahouse culture originated in the Southern Song Dynasty (1127-1279). After the Jin people (an ethnic minority in North China who established the Jin Dynasty during 1115-1234) overthrew the Northern Song Dynasty (960-1127), the Southern Song Dynasty established its capital in Hangzhou. The Confucian tradition and culture of the central plains spread to the city, where tea markets and teahouses prospered. Hangzhou teahouses proudly display seasonal flowers and famous paintings. They sell excellent tea, soup, and wine throughout the year, including seven-treasure *leicha* tea, fried dough twists, *yangutang* tea in winter, and *meihua* (plum blossom) wine in summer.

Thus, we can see that the custom of combining paintings and calligraphy in Hangzhou teahouses and various popular drinking methods were developed as far back as the Southern

77

🍵 *West Lake scene*

Song Dynasty. *Leicha* tea, a health drink made of pounded tea leaves, fried sesame, fried peanuts, fried (uncooked) rice grains or puffed rice, could work up an appetite. The *Yangutang* tea referred to might be *yandou* tea now popular in Zhejiang Province. It was a common practice to add onions and ginger to tea during the Song Dynasty.

The present teahouses in the Wu-Yue area are fewer than those in Sichuan Province because most of the Zhejiang people drink tea at home. However, the cultural atmosphere of Hangzhou tearooms is much stronger.

The Hangzhou teahouses have several features, one of which is the use of outstanding sources of water, and tasting it in an excellent environment, thus achieving the true objective of tea art. Hangzhou tearooms are most noted for their genuineness. *Longjing* tea is regarded as the best tea in Hangzhou. The best-quality *longjing* tea is hard to come by, for it does not originate in Longjing Village but from Lion Peak. However, in Hangzhou people can taste the super-fine or first-grade *longjing* tea. It is classified as a green tea, which keeps tea's natural color. A cup of *longjing* tea is a work of art with its clear tea water, beautiful leaf buds, and mild and sweet taste similar to that of sweet, clear morning dew. Good quality water is of vital importance. Water from the Hupao Spring is regarded as the best; the water quality in other areas, while inferior, is still much better than those of inland waters. People greatly enjoy themselves visiting the West Lake and Temple of Inspired Seclusion, and drinking first-grade *longjing* tea with water from the Hupao Spring. The inherent charm lies in the fact that both tea and water keep their original color, fragrance, taste and natural qualities wherever people drink, in pavilions, terraces and open halls, or in lush mountain valleys.

🍵 *Hupao Spring*

In Hangzhou, most tearooms are elegant, simple, and unsophisticated. Few are like the teahouses in Beijing and Tianjin, which combine *shuochang* (a genre of popular entertainment including mainly talking and singing) and *quyi* (Chinese folk art forms). A few adopt the practice of drinking tea with refreshments and rice porridge common in Guangzhou and

78

Hong Kong teahouses. Hangzhou teahouses are sometimes simply referred to as tearooms because of their elegant, quiet, and beautiful artistic conception. Small shops attached to the tearooms sell handiworks such as Hangzhou fans, bamboo carvings, small images of Ji Gong, or West Lake lotus root starch.

People feel that they become one with the West Lake and the sky overhead when they drink tea in the tearooms along the Su and Bai causeways; when they appreciate

 West Lake morning

the gurgling Hupao Spring and its folk stories, they can sense the wonderful aesthetic atmosphere. When they drink *longjing* tea while listening to the gurgling spring and the clear and melodious sound of bells, watching the wreaths of incense smoke and the devoted Buddhists chanting in the Temple of Inspired Seclusion, visitors will realize the truth of Buddhist allegorical words or gestures even if they themselves are not Buddhists. People can truly experience the cultural essence of tea in Hangzhou not only because of the methods of brewing and making tea, but also because of the historic atmosphere. The beautiful scenery of Hangzhou provides an excellent natural environment for the development of the tearooms by the West Lake.

Hangzhou is itself a large, natural "teahouse." Tea integrates naturally with man, heaven and earth, mountains and rivers, cloud and mists, bamboo and stones, and flowers and trees. Humanity and nature, tea culture and Wu-Yue culture also share each others characteristics. Local teahouses also have the function of settling civil disputes. When both sides agree, they may go to a teahouse to settle the dispute in public. Even if they arrive initially opposing one another, the two parties have to speak in a mild tone. The losing side will have to pay for tea, which is called *chipincha*. The parties are able to distinguish clearly between right and wrong without hurting each other, a clear manifestation of the Golden Mean of Confucianism and the theory of governing by doing nothing that is against nature.

Tianjin became a city after the Jin and Yuan dynasties to service the Great Canal. It has been an important industrial and commercial metropolis in North China in modern times.

79

Because it is a port city as well as being close to Beijing, Tianjin teahouses imitated those in Beijing to meet the needs of industrial and commercial development, as well as those of ordinary people.

As in the large Beijing teahouses, the Tianjin teahouses sold refreshments, accompanied by the singing of operas, storytelling, and *dagu* (a versified story sung to the accompaniment of a small drum and other instruments). Every customer was served with a teapot and cup, while groups of customers were provided with teapots and several cups. People of various trades drank tea while enjoying their refreshments amid the entertainment. Some of them came to teahouses to look for jobs, such as lacquering, bricklaying, and woodworking. Teahouses were also often antique trading floors. In the *Sandexuan* Teahouse, craftsmen drank tea and looked for jobs in the morning, while at noon, storytelling and *dagu* were performed. Unlike Beijing teahouses, which were carefully classified, Sichuan teahouses, or Hangzhou tearooms, which have their unique local features, most of the Tianjin teahouses met the needs of business and commerce from different parts of China.

🍵 *Teahouse, painted in the early Republican period*

In the old days, customers in Tianjin restaurants would be greeted with a cup of top-grade tea as soon as they arrived so that they could refresh themselves and whet their appetite. After that, formal courses would be served. Tea would be served again after the meal so that customers could rest for a while before leaving. It was a good tradition. In such a way, Tianjin teahouses gave full play to the social and economic development of the city. The old local residents drank tea three times a day. The cultural atmosphere of the teahouses, however, was not strong, which was a common characteristic of the teahouses in North China.

However, the teahouses in Shanghai, another modern industrial and commercial metropolis, possessed a stronger cultural atmosphere. In the past, the tearooms in gardens were often filled with guests and friends. Many sons and daughters of the rich went to tearooms to learn civilized behavior and mingle with men of letters and scholars and to pose as lovers of culture. Although, compared with Beijing teahouses where tea was served without refreshments, Shanghai tearooms possessed less of a literary atmosphere; they could be regarded as learned and refined places. The typical teahouse with local features was situated in

 Shanghai Quan'an Teahouse, Republican period

the old Chenghuangmiao (City God Temple) area. For example, in the old *Deyilou* Teahouse, the customers on the ground floor were small tradesmen, porters and other laborers, and the stalls by the front gate sold sesame cakes. The second floor, where customers drank tea while listening to storytelling, had a greater cultural atmosphere, and the third floor, where bird connoisseurs gathered, was full of vibrancy and the joy of life. The most quietly and tastefully laid out tearoom was situated in *Yuyuan* Garden, bordering *Chenghuangmiao*. Though inferior to Suzhou gardens, the traditional zigzag-shaped southern private garden was very beautiful. The tearooms close to ponds and bamboo groves were very elegant. Shanghai people called teahouses *fuchaguan* to express their longing for leisure.

81

Yuyuan Garden, near the old Chenghuangmiao, Shanghai

The teahouses in Guangzhou, a sprawling city situated next to the Pearl River in southern China, were even grander. The local people called simply called their breakfast *zaocha* (literally, morning-tea). If a Cantonese said "I would like to invite you to drink tea tomorrow," he was simply expressing a euphemism for inviting you to a meal. The old Guangdong tearooms were inexpensive. Regular customers would be served with a cup of tea, and two steamed buns stuffed with diced grilled pork, steamed dumplings with the dough gathered at the top, or dumplings stuffed with shrimp.

🍵 *A small teahouse in the countryside of southern China*

Some small village teahouses in Guangdong resembled waterside pavilions with bamboo or wood bark fences. Others were situated in the hills or nestled against mountains overlooking the city. Customers were served with a cup of tea with thick stalks and large leaves, and two steamed dumplings with the dough gathered at the top, but compared with the teahouses in Guangzhou and Hong Kong, they had a stronger cultural and more artistic ambience.

Though not as learned and refined as the tearooms by the West Lake in Hangzhou, the simple and unadorned teahouses were full of the appeal of waterside villages. The villagers drank tea three times a day in the waterside teahouses. In the morning, they appreciated the rising sun and misty morning; at noon, the passing boats setting sails or sculling; in the evening, the moon rising in the east, which was reflected in the water. The waterside teahouses in Guangdong were called *tancha*, which simply meant, to enjoy tea. People could learn tea's taste, and the joys and sorrows of life. Compared with the teahouses in large cities, they were rich in the philosophies of life and nature.

Beijing teahouses epitomized the advantages of other local teahouses, and were noted for their great variety and rich sense of culture. Historically, there were many kinds of Beijing teahouses, including *dachaguan* (great teahouses), *qingchaguan* (those serving tea only), *shuchaguan* (teahouses where storytelling was performed), *erhunpu* (teahouses selling tea, wine, and dinners), *hongluguan* (teahouses installed with red stoves), and *yechaguan* (teahouses in the country). There were also innumerable tea stalls and booths. The teahouses became the meeting place for people from all walks of life. It was more convenient for people to carry out activities in teahouses than in formal halls or restaurants, for, first and foremost, it was less expensive to simply enjoy tea than to order a full meal, and besides, one felt more at ease meeting friends in a teahouse than at home. Strangers without families could also relax in teahouses. Teahouses became popular because of the special composition of the population. Therefore, teahouses of various forms and with varied functions spread all over Beijing.

🍵 *Teahouses in Beijing were noted for their rich sense of culture (Lao She Teahouse)*

Novels of the Ming and Qing dynasties occupy an important place in the history of Chinese literature. Classical Chinese novels, especially full-length masterpieces, were not written solely in the writers' studies, but were revised according to story-tellers' scripts over the years. In other words, they became a type of oral literature of the performers in teahouses or restaurants. Such masterpieces included *The Romance of Three Kingdoms* and *Outlaws of the Marsh*. Because such Chinese novels took root among the masses, they displayed a greater vitality than other literary works. Teahouse culture during the Song and Yuan dynasties up until the Ming and Qing dynasties made a special contribution to the development of the novel, and Beijing *shuchaguan* was the best evidence of this method of development.

Tea and Chinese Culture

In the old days, there were many *shuchaguan* in Beijing, where tea was a secondary consideration, and people came there mainly to listen to the stories. Storytelling was performed two times a day: from 3:00pm to about 6:00pm, and from about 8:00pm to 11:00pm or even 12:00am! Sometimes the storytelling started one or two hours earlier, providing opportunities for ordinary performers to practice. Before the performance started, tea was served without refreshments so that patrons could simply relax and quench their thirst. After the storytelling began, the teahouses only received customers who listened to it in its entirety. Customers would refresh themselves with tea while listening. The bill was called "payment for storytelling" instead of payment for tea because customers went to the teahouses to listen to storytelling, while tea played only a supplementary role.

Famous *shuchaguan* were exquisitely furnished with cane or wooden tables and chairs, and decorated with works of calligraphy and paintings to create an atmosphere appropriate for storytelling. A teahouse would invite a storyteller to perform well in advance. A long story would last two or three months. The teahouse took 30 percent of the income, while the storyteller received 70 percent. As an intellectual, the storyteller was greatly respected by the teahouse manager. There were all kinds of stories, including historical stories, such as *The Romances of Three Kingdoms, Journey to the West, Records of the Eastern and Western Han dynasties*, and *Romance of the Sui and Tang dynasties; Tales of Magistrate Bao*, and stories about gods and spirits, such as *The Biography of Lord Ji*, and *The Romance of the Canonized Gods*, and *Liaozhai Zhiyi*, which was full of strange tales as well as beautiful love stories. Customers enjoyed themselves listening to the interesting stories about gods and spirits told by excellent story-tellers, who expanded the meanings of the stories to illustrate the fickleness of the world.

Lord Ji

Various *quyi* (Chinese folk art forms) were performed in the *shuchaguan* in the Tianqiao area; they included *meihua dagu, lihua dagu,* and storytelling in Beijing and Tangshan dialects with drum accompaniment. The stories were either taken from voluminous storytelling books or newly-compiled in order to be fashionable and to suit the contemporary environment.

84

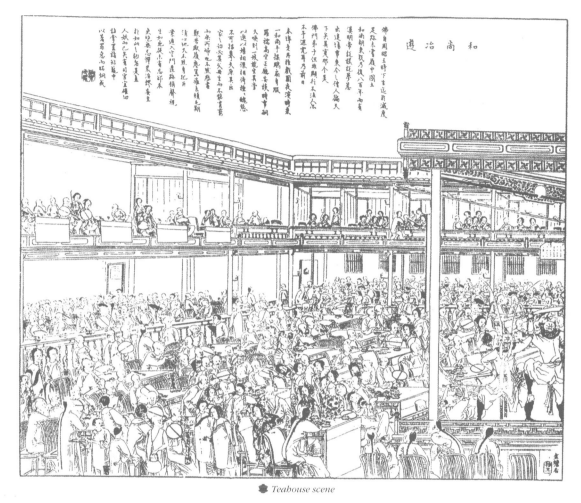

佛自周昭王時下生於娑婆

足臨末當度中閻王

和兩朝東敗万後八百年而有

漢明帝於後漢孝章

出迎遇事東合見佛人編天

下天真貴邪个吳

佛門弟子但雜聞利本法介衆

不平深究其乃前日

本身支聲雜戲圖夜演時東

一和兩卡撻聘麻身服

羅猪高堂正廳安眠事調

大喚到一般龍安芙芽

以邊以掯相親情獲禮晚慈

不可話蒙夫原其花

宜口記火蓋父母言切不鮮育害

山來兩湖吐本照愿害

聚落獻飯鹿堂幕五領光期

清口吧几太州能記日

蒙道八子門進路稍聲相

生知免援小有岳印來

成泡無心押長淮紙疊皇

科枳如己髯有司宣宣確切

人妖如乙氣貴小動當蓋皇

以若蜀葛忍幼聞蛋洞咸

和尚冶遺

85

Teahouse scene

Though *shuchaguan* had a strong atmosphere of folk culture, there were many *qingchaguan* in Beijing, providing places for people from all walks of life to entertain themselves elegantly. Tea was served without accompanying refreshments in these teahouses. Most were simply furnished with elegant square tables and wooden chairs, and teacups with covers were used. In spring, summer and autumn, a shelter would be set outside or in the courtyard of the teahouse. The seats in the front shelter were for ordinary customers, while those in the room were for regular customers. Comfortable seats were set in the courtyard. Wooden signboards with characters such as *maojian, yuqian, queshe,* and *dafang* were hung in front of the gate or under the roof of the shelter to show that the teahouse was selling first-class tea.

The teahouses opened at five every morning. Residents of old Peking were accustomed to getting up early to do exercises, which were called *liuzao*. They would go for a walk in quiet places with their birds in cages, and then do exercises by the banks of the reed marshes or on the banks of a moat. Once they had decided they had breathed in enough fresh air, they would return to the town and go to the teahouses. They would hang the birdcages nearby and drink tea while appreciating the birds' calls. The trained larks, babblers, *hongdian, landian* and other species could call in more than 10 ways, and imitate the cries of magpies, titmice, hawks, cuckoos, and wild geese. The old customers then talked about their experiences of cultivating tea and keeping pets, engaged in small talk, or commented on current events. They developed a unique method of integrating tea and nature. The shopkeepers of *qingchaguan* helped well-known pet keepers to organize *chaniaohui* (parties to appreciate both tea and birds) to solicit customers. They would send invitation cards on fancy stationery and red envelopes to old customers, and put up posters on the street. The pet keepers would go to the parties and old customers took pleasure in admiring them, while teahouses could reap great profit in the process. In winter, besides warming themselves and chatting in teahouses, customers liked to appreciate butterflies spreading their wings, and watch cricket fighting; activities which added vitality to the bleak winter, and made their lives more colorful. It was a unique scene in Beijing. In the afternoon, these old customers were replaced by businessmen and merchants, who negotiated their business at teahouses.

There were also *qichaguan* in Beijing, where customers played chess. *Qichaguan* were simply furnished with timber or lumps of wood painted with chessboards, which were partly buried in the ground, or chessboards with benches on both sides. More than 10 customers would drink tea in a *qichaguan* while playing chess each afternoon. People of Beijing in old times, even the poor, had refined hobbies. *Qichaguan* was an example. When they played chess while drinking scented tea or other ordinary tea, the chessboard was like a battlefield of life, and they would temporarily forget about their sufferings. Because of this quality, tea was also called *Wangyoujun* (worry-free).

People went to *Yechaguan* (teahouses in the country) and seasonal tea sheds for outings to

🏮 *Teahouse in Beijing*

appreciate beautiful gardens in an outdoor setting. People of Beijing in old times loved going for outings. They went out to enjoy the beautiful scenery in spring, in summer to appreciate the lotus flowers, in autumn the maple leaves, and in winter the Western Hills shimmering with snow. Some old people loved the melon sheds, beanpoles, vineyards, and fishponds on the outskirts of the city, so *yechaguan* appeared in these beautiful areas. For example, the *Maizi Teashop* at Chaoyangmenwai was established in a peaceful and secluded place surrounded by reeds and many ponds. Skillful fish farmers often went there to net water fleas. When the sun was sinking in the west, old men walked on crisscross footpaths between the fields, and gathered at the teahouse. The teahouse at Liupukang was surrounded by melon sheds and beanpoles.

Customers could appreciate rustic sights such as the flowers of cucumbers and eggplants, and butterflies, just as Lu Fangweng (Lu You) had taken great pleasure in chatting about the cultivation of mulberries and hemp with old farmers. People recovered their original simplicity in such an environment. The Vineyard Teahouse at Chaoyangmenwai was close to a clear stream flowing to the west, while ponds lay to the east and south and many grape trellises and towering old trees surrounded by low fences to the north. Scholars often went there to play chess, solve riddles or write poems.

Good-quality water was rare in Beijing, and most of the city water was bitter. The Qing Palaces took water from the sweet and refreshing spring at the Jade Spring Hill in the northwest part of Beijing. Because of the poor quality city water it was best to build *yechaguan* in beautiful places near excellent natural springs. The *Shanglong* and *Xialong* teahouses at Andingmenwai were such teahouses. They were only about 100 paces apart. The Prosperity Temple was situated there in the Qing Dynasty, with dozens of tranquil ponds to the north. When the 300-year-old "memorial tree to King Wen" blossomed, the fragrance spread all over the courtyard. There was also a well with sweet, refreshing, and clear water outside the temple. Rich with cultural relics, beautiful views and excellent water, it was an excellent place to drink tea. The shopkeeper built a canopy near the well to sell tea, wine, and steamed buns. The teahouse was a small earthen structure standing on the slope.

The teahouses by the Gaoliangqiao and Baishiqiao bridges flourished because pleasure-boats passed there during the Qing Dynasty. *Yechaguan,* known as quiet spots away from the noisy city, enlivened the people's life and added natural interest to the process of tea-drinking. Although not as secluded and quiet as the teahouses by the West Lake in Hangzhou, they were simple and unadorned and, thus, closer to the true spiritual qualities of the Chinese tea ceremony.

Such teahouses also included seasonal tea sheds in parks. The most famous ones were situated at Little Western Heaven by the North Lake, in which lotuses grew. Almond tea, mashed peas and *suzao* meat were also served.

People had social contacts in *Dachaguan* (great teahouses) with catering services. The old Beijing *dachaguan* had various functions. They served tea and food, and provided excellent service to people in various trades, such as businessmen and scholars. In *Teahouse,* the famous work written by Lao She, the old Beijing *dachaguan* is portrayed vividly.

The *Lao She Teahouse* at Qianmen has carried on the tradition and opened a way for those who follow. *Dachaguan* became popular because of their multiple functions and good service.

Tianhuixuan Teahouse at Di'anmenwai was the most famous of the old Beijing *dachaguan*; *Huifengxuan* Teahouse at Donganmenwai was second only to it.

The teahouses were tastefully furnished. The first counter at the entrance was responsible for orders to go; the middle counter connected with the front and back halls. Each counter received different types of customers. In some *dachaguan,* the back and middle halls were connected with each other while, in other teahouses, the halls were separated by a courtyard.

The teahouses served customers with exquisite tea sets. Teacups with covers kept the tea ready and warm. A strong sense of etiquette was always practiced while drinking tea. They used the covers of teacups to stir tea and cover their mouths. Waiters would take good care of customers' tea sets and seats so that they could continue to drink after lunch.

In terms of service, the Beijing *dachaguan* also included *hongluguan*

🍵 *The teahouses served customers with exquisite tea sets*

(teahouses installed with red stoves), *wowoguan* (teahouses serving tea with refreshments), and *banhuguan* (teahouses installed with a large copper pot). The differences between these classes of teahouses included the following:

Hongluguan were installed with red stoves which baked Chinese as well as Manchu-style pastries. A wide variety of pastries and snack items were served.

Wowoguan served various refreshments, including *aiwowo,* steamed sponge cakes, *paicha, pengao,* and sesame seed cakes.

Characterized by a large copper pot, *banhuguan* suited both refined and popular tastes.

Tea and Chinese Culture

Erhunpu served tea without refreshments, but provided dining facilities where customers could choose from a provided menu, or even bring in their own food to be cooked to order.

Dachaguan had many functions—people could drink tea, dine, make social contacts, and entertain themselves there. They were broader in scope, and had a more profound influence than other teahouses. The *Lao She Teahouse* is still popular among people from all walks of life today, and the teahouse tradition, long thought to have died out in contemporary China, is gaining new popularity. Tea acted as a medium of contact and had a great social function in the realm of the *dachaguan*. Slowly, the culture of the traditional teahouse is returning to China.

🍵 *Tea and entertainment.*　　　　　🍵 *Opposite: Lao She Teahouse, Beijing*

Chapter 6

6. Tea and Chinese Art

Chinese tea culture came into being at the height of the Tang Dynasty, and paintings featuring tea as a central theme appeared at about the same time. However, tea paintings of this time, like other paintings depicting banquet scenes or scenes of people drinking, displayed tea though they did not attempt to capture its spiritual essence and aesthetic qualities. In *The Book of Tea* by Lu Yu, there were tea paintings, but they merely showed the process of brewing tea for practical knowledge. In a sense, such paintings were simply like advertising a new type of food. But many poets and calligraphers counted themselves among the tea drinking population. Headed by Lu Yu, many composed beautiful poems while enjoying tea in social situations. This aroused later generations to associate art with tea, and made later painters and calligraphers contemplate the arts whenever enjoying tea.

Xiao Yi Contemplating the Masterpiece of Lan Ting by Strategy by Yan Liben, made in the Tang Dynasty, is the earliest known tea painting. It shows one Confucian scholar and two Buddhist monks drinking tea together. On the right of the picture, the scholar and the monks are talking about their philosophy and religion as they wait for their tea. On the left, two servants, one old and one young, are involved in brewing the tea with single-minded determination. The old servant is putting the teapot on the stove and brewing tea elaborately, while the young one is holding a bowl, waiting to present the brewed tea to his master. With the expressions of the characters being true to life, the painting is a meticulous work, reflecting

🍵 *Yan Liben: Xiao Yi Contemplating the Masterpiece of Lan Ting by Strategy (Tang Dynasty)*

the simple way that scholars and monks often drank together. Such a work set a powerful precedent in that tea painting should not only display the material life of tea brewing and drinking, but should express some thought behind the philosophy of tea. The painting is pregnant with meaning in that both Confucians and Buddhists talked about philosophical and religious doctrine as they drank tea. It clearly shows that talking about tea was more important than brewing tea.

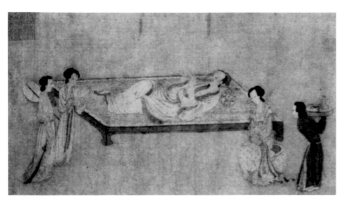

🐦 *Zhang Xuan: Ausiciousness and Happiness (Tang Dynasty)*

The painting *Auspiciousness and Happiness* displayed Emperor Minghuang of the Tang Dynasty drinking tea. In the painting, the Emperor lies on his bed, with three female servants standing beside it. Another servant is holding a tea set containing tea and fruit, and it appears that the Emperor has just finished drinking tea and has ordered her to clear away the tea set. Judging from the tea sets, some specialists in tea think that this painting shows the way of making tea with loose leaves in the early Tang Dynasty. But culturally, we pay more attention to the two words "Auspiciousness and Happiness," which was what the painter tried to express.

The anonymous painting, *Palace Music,* shows the grand scene of imperial ladies drinking tea. In the palace is a grand table upon which was a large bowl to hold the brewed tea together with a ladle for serving. The serving maids are all holding musical instruments. Their clothes display beautiful colors, and their hair is arranged in buns high on their heads. They sit on refined embroidered seats, some holding a bowl with both hands and drinking tea, others playing the four-stringed Chinese lute, *or Xiao* (similar to a bamboo flute, but held vertically),

🐦 *Anonymous: Palace Music (Tang Dynasty)*

or other classic musical instruments. Some serving maids are standing in attendance, while a cat is lying under the table.

Overall, during the Tang Dynasty, which was the pioneering stage of tea paintings, painters depicted the details and scenes of tea brewing and drinking concretely and minutely, but they did not show the spiritual connotation of tea in any meaningful way. After all, this opened up a new field for tea culture. By visible artistic means, people not only realized the effects of tea, but also began to heed its spiritual experience as conveyed through works of art.

From the Five Dynasties to the Song Dynasty, tea paintings were rich in content. They displayed either large tea banquets of palaces and officialdom, or scholars drinking tea in their studies, or the common people appraising and drinking tea. As most were painted by famous painters, the artistic level of tea painting was further raised.

Such a painting was *Han Xizai Attending an Evening Banquet,* painted by Gu Hongzhong during the Five Dynasties period. The painting depicts a large tea banquet. In it there are many vividly-displayed figures drinking tea as women are dancing. Two maidservants are

Gu Hogzhong: Han Xizai Attending an Evening Banquet (Five Dynasties)

holding plates, on which the utensils look much like those in the painting *Auspiciousness and Happiness.*

Emperor Huizong of the Northern Song Dynasty was an accomplished artist. He had a good knowledge of chess, calligraphy, painting, and *qin* (a seven-stringed plucked instrument in some ways similar to the zither). He especially liked tea art. His painting *Scholars' Gathering* depicts a tea banquet. In a noble garden with a pool, mountain stones and willows, there is a big square table, on which are fruit, refreshments, and tea. Around the table are more than ten scholars. At the lower corner on the left some servants are brewing tea, with tea sets, the stove, and the big basket for storing the tea sets for future use clearly shown. All elements are

Emperor Huizong: Scholars' Gathering (Northern Song Dynasty)

Liu Songnian: *Rumpling Tea (Southern Song Dynasty)*

98

Liu Songnian: *Gambling Market in the Tea Plantation*
(Southern Song Dynasty)

clear and recognizable. Behind the tea table, between the flowers and trees, is another table, on which there are an incense burner and a *qin*. This showed that scholars had made tea drinking an elegant affair, not excluding music on the lute and the fragrance of the flowers.

In terms of achievements in art, the tea paintings by Liu Songnian of the Southern Song Dynasty hold the highest place of honor. Liu's paintings, which have been passed down as a gift through the centuries, include *Rumpling Tea* (showing the tea art of the Song Dynasty), *Gambling Market in the Tea Plantation,* and *Lu Tong Brewing Tea.* The last two paintings, in particular, have both profound implications and are great achievements in art.

The painting *Gambling Market in the Tea Plantation,* for example, depicts the appraisal of tea among the common people. In it all the people, old and young, including women and children, have vivid expressions. The scene of appraisal of tea in a tea producing area is full of life. On the left a woman with a child is selling tea in her basket; in the middle a street vendor, with two baskets of tea on his shoulder pole, is also selling tea; on the right gamblers are appraising tea, which is the main theme of the painting. On either basket containing tea and tea sets on an old man's shoulder pole is a tag, on which is written, "First-Class River Tea." Men, women, and children all focus their attention on those appraising tea on the right, a detail which makes the theme "appraising tea" more prominent. The people appraising tea all have individual tea sets. This painting shows the appraisal of tea among common people in the Song Dynasty. Vivid, detailed, and true to life, it is both a masterpiece of art and a precious reference material for the study of the history of tea drinking.

Another work of Liu's entitled *Lu Tong Brewing Tea,* is vividly painted according to a poem on drinking tea written by Lu Tong, a poet during the Tang Dynasty. The painting depicts scholars drinking tea under the moon by mountain stones and bamboo groves. It reflects the experience and happiness of people drinking tea. It deserves to be particularly noted, for it is a portrayal of tea art which approaches and emphasizes the role of nature.

🫖 *Qian Xuan: Lu Tong Brewing Tea (Song Dynasty)*

It can be seen from the tea paintings by Liu Songnian that in the Southern Song Dynasty tea culture influenced all walks of life and further increased its role in society and culture.

In the Song Dynasty there were other paintings reflecting scholars drinking tea in their studies. For example, in the anonymous painting *Characters,* a scholar sits up straight in his study, where *qin*, books, and paintings are placed on the desk, flowers are arranged in the middle of the table, and a stove is set up on the right. With the charcoal fire roaring, a young servant is carefully boiling water for tea. It is truly a leisurely and elegant scene.

🫖 *Anonymous: Characters (Song Dynasty)*

99

The painting *Children Playing in Spring* by Su Hanchen of the Song Dynasty, shows many children tuning the *qin*, practicing calligraphy, playing games, and tasting tea. It has the rich flavor of life and implies the strong bond of friendship between children.

Su Hanchen: Children Playing in Spring (Song Dynasty)

In all, the Song Dynasty ushered in a great achievement in the advancement of tea-themed paintings.

In the Yuan and Ming dynasties, tea culture had two characteristics. One was that it had deeper philosophical meaning, advocating agreement with nature and blending with mountains and waters, heaven and earth, and the cosmos. The other was that tea drinking among common people was developed, and that the friendship and harmony of tea drinkers deeply influenced all manner of people. Excellent tea paintings in the Yuan and Ming dynasties also reflected these two aspects.

However, in contrast, painters at that time paid more attention to the connotation of tea paintings than to techniques of tea culture. This conforms to the overall trend in the development of Chinese tea culture. After the Yuan and Ming dynasties, the Chinese feudal culture became mature, and social and ideological conflicts became sharper, making tea paintings at that time more profound.

Appraising Tea was painted by Zhao Mengfu after *Gambling Market in the Tea Plantation* by Liu Songnian in the Song Dynasty. The former attached more importance to the theme of appraising tea, and emphasized the psychological relationship

Zhao Mengfu: Appraising Tea (Ming Dynasty)

among the four central figures in the latter by painting them in minute detail. In the painting, *Lu Yu Tasting Tea,* by Zhao Yuan, we see that unlike people in the Tang and Song dynasties who drank tea in studies, courtyards, or palaces, people drank tea in mountains, near streams, or in fields, which reflected their attempt to communicate with nature.

In the Ming Dynasty, Zhu Quan, the 17th son of Emperor Taizu, further developed Chinese tea art, and became a main representative of naturalist tea drinkers. Owing to political frustration and seemingly never-ending conflict, he became a hermit and devoted himself to founding the naturalistic tea ceremony. Since then, many similarly frustrated scholars have followed him. Among them were poets and painters. For example, the painting *Brewing Tea in Yuchuan* by Ding Yunpeng depicts the scene of tasting tea on a mountain beside banana trees under bamboo groves. Wen Zhengming and Tang Yin (Bohu) of the "four outstanding people in Wuzhong" during the reign of Emperor Jiajing, all painted similar tea paintings. Wen Zhengming's paintings—*Lu Yu Brewing Tea, Tasting Tea,* and *Tea Gathering in the Huishan Mountain*—all stress hiding in high mountains and amid bamboo groves, while Tang Yin's painting *Qin Player* and two paintings entitled *Tasting Tea* are clear, grandiose, and varied. All these are fine examples of tea painting.

In the Ming Dynasty, many scholars painted tea painting, tasted tea in their studies, or drank tea together

Ding Yunpeng: Brewing Tea in Yuchuan (Ming Dynasty)

in bedchambers. All these reflected certain living conditions and the wide use of tea among common scholars, but, compared with Tang Yin, Wen Zhengming, and others, they are not as significant ideologically or artistically. However, many illustrations in the collected works and novels of the Ming Dynasty, such as the painting of tasting tea in the courtyard, the painting of a lady tasting tea in her boudoir, and the painting of tasting tea on a boat in a river surrounded by green lotus leaves, reflect the vivid tea culture and the broad social walks of life for those who engaged in it. The painting *Sweeping Away Snow and Brewing Tea* from the novel *The Plum in the Golden Vase* depicts figures and the scene vividly.

🍵 *Len Mei: Enjoying the Moon (Qing Dynasty)*

In the Qing Dynasty the tradition of tea paintings continued. Since the ways of making tea were by then well established, tea paintings now attached greater importance to items such as tea cups, tea pots, and scenes of nature which emphasized the social aspects of tea life. In particular, tea paintings at the height of the period, during the reigns of the Kangxi and Qianlong Emperors, reflected this harmony and liveliness. For example, the painting *Spring Market at Peace* by Ding Guanpeng during the reign of Qianlong depicts scholars who are tasting fragrant tea under pine and plum trees along a broad and beautiful expanse of green grass, together with an old man selling tea and fruit passing by with two baskets on his shoulder pole. The painting *Enjoying the Moon* by Leng Mei in the Qing Dynasty depicts the enjoyment of contemplating the moon while tasting tea in the garden. Tea drinking among common people in the Qing Dynasty was also very popular, a fact reflected in paintings. For example, Yangliuqing woodcuts portray ladies playing cards while tasting tea. Besides this type of work, paintings

Yangliuqing woodcut of the Qing Dynasty

on appraising tea after Liu Songnian's works and books on the art of tea painting by Lu Tong were often seen.

During the Republican Period (1912-1949), civic tea culture was practiced on a large scale, and works of art on teahouses naturally followed. Tea paintings in books on the art of painting, as well as tea illustrations in novels, were by now nothing new.

Since the Tang Dynasty, tea was a major subject of painters, who produced many noteworthy works. The special character of tea made it an important way for painters to express their thoughts and feelings. These tea paintings simultaneously inspired tea culture itself, reflecting tea art and the tea ceremony in visible forms and deepening people's understanding of its inner secrets.

103

Mastering Chinese calligraphy is not merely a matter of technical skill, but also requires the interpretation of and ability to convey the essence of life in how the character—a reflection of the human spirit—is formed. The calligrapher's skill holds the key to life's vital energy. Many calligraphers feel that good calligraphic work not only represents a skill gained through long-term cultivation of thought, but also has a lot to do with the state of mind of the artist at the time of writing. Tea can keep people sober-minded and make them feel as if they are filling the cosmos with their thoughts. Perhaps just because of this special relationship between tea and calligraphy, many calligraphers like drinking tea. Thus, tea calligraphy, which took poems about tea or the word "tea" as its subject, became a special preference of painters and calligraphers. Many famous calligraphers had "tea copybooks," or wrote poems on tea in calligraphic form as a way of expressing their art and thoughts.

Tea formed an aesthetic association with the art of calligraphy very early on. Early in the period when Lu Yu created the primary system of Chinese tea culture and compiled *The Book of Tea*, calligraphers took an active part in tea culture activities. Yan Zhenqing, Lu Yu's good friend despite their great difference in age, was well-known as the originator of Yan-style calligraphy. Quite a lot of people knew that Yan was a famous calligrapher, but did not know his official rank or political achievements. After Confucian Yan Zhenqing made friends with hermit Lu Yu and monk Jiao Ran in Huzhou, they cooperated with each other in many respects, and advocated the combination of tea with calligraphy for the first time. Take the famous Three-Gui Pavilion for example. The pavilion was named for its building on the date, month and year of gui, one of the ten Heavenly branches. In Taoism the word "three" implies "bearing everything on earth," while Lu, Jiao, and Yan were three persons. Lu Yu designed the pavilion, Jiao Ran wrote a poem to serve as an inscription, and Yan Zhenqing engraved its history on a stone tablet. These were called "three superb works" of art. Thus, from the Tang Dynasty, calligraphy on tea officially became an important part of Chinese culture as well as tea culture.

🌸 *Yan Zhenqing and his calligraphy*

104

🌸 *The famous Three-Gui Pavilion in Huzhou*

In the Song Dynasty, Emperor Huizong liked tea, poems, and calligraphy. He wrote *An Exposition on Tea* together with various essays on tea, painted tea paintings, or inscribed poems on tea paintings with the special artistic temperament of a calligrapher. His calligraphy was known as the "thin gold" style. From his painting *Scholars' Gathering*, a superb work of art combining paintings,

🌸 *The "thin gold" style calligraphy of Emperor Huizong*

poetry, calligraphy, and the image of a lavish tea banquet, we can see his inscribed poems together with those of his ministers.

Zheng Banqiao

In the Ming Dynasty, Tang Yin and Wen Zhengming had a good command of tea art, poems, and paintings. Here Zheng Banqiao, of the Qing Dynasty, is particularly noteworthy. He was also called Zheng Xie, with the courtesy name of Kerou. Born in Xinghua, Jiangsu Province, Zheng was a famous calligrapher, painter, and poet, and was, therefore, called a truly superb person in three aspects. He was especially expert at painting orchids, black bamboo, and peculiarly-shaped stones, and his brushstrokes were beautiful and vigorous. His poems strived for realism, freedom, and generosity, while his calligraphy blended official script, regular script, cursive script, and grass script. He was also a great lover of tea. In his poem *Prefecture Chief Presenting Tea to Me When I Lived in Yanzhou*, he wrote: "This quality tea was given to you by the late ministers Cai Xiang and Ding Wei in Heaven; How should I have thought that you would present it to me?"

Owing to the special relationship between tea and calligraphy, many great calligraphers wrote special books on calligraphy for the purpose of tea appreciation. Some people collected examples of calligraphy to compile a book for their own comparative study. For example, they gathered various examples of tea calligraphy taken from *Xuanmi Tower, Explanation and Study of Principles of Composition of Characters,* as well as works written by such famous calligraphers as Yan Zhenqing, Mi Fu, Xu Wei, Su Guo,

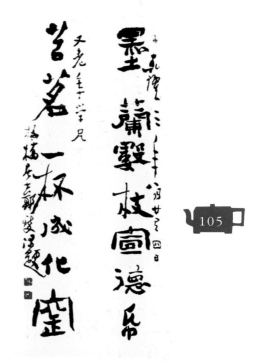

105

Calligraphy of Zheng Banqiao

Calligraphy of Xu Wei

Dong Qichang, Zhang Ruitu, Wang Tingjian, Wu Changshuo, Zhao Mengfu, and Zheng Banqiao together in a book on tea calligraphy.

There were many tales about tea in different parts of China. Some of the authors of these tales told of the origin of famous teas with a view to both adding romance to the teas and to making them more exalted while at the same time publicizing the beauty and prosperity of their hometowns. China was vast in territory and rich in resources, but almost nothing was universally liked by everyone and eulogized in different tales except tea and liquor. There were tales about grains and plants, such as the tales about the "Goddess of Flowers", and the "Silkworm Lady Meeting Qiu Hu in the Mulberry Garden". Tea stories, however, were more specific. All famous teas had their own graceful and romantic legends, through which people eulogized famous mountains and rivers, thus making them yearn for and admire famous teas all the more. Tea planters were good at making advertisements for their fine teas through legends. The origin of famous teas accounted for a large proportion of the legends about tea, and every famous tea seemed to have a wonderful history.

Maofeng tea of Huangshan, Anhui Province, is one famous kind of tea in China, and its Tunxi green tea is praised by many as "green gold." The first-class Tunxi green tea is also called "treasure of teas," about which there is a beautiful love story: once there was orphan girl named Luo Xiang who lived at the foot of Huangshan Mountain. The girl, as beautiful as one could imagine, picked tea while singing beautiful songs in a melodious voice. High officials, noble lords, scholars, sons of wealthy

"Tunxi green" Maofeng tea

men, and rich businessmen all proposed marriage to her. Troubled by this, Luo Xiang told all the villagers and her admirers that she would be engaged by using the "treasure of teas" she had picked. This puzzled everyone, and one morning, at the foot of Huangshan Mountain, all the townspeople gathered. Luo Xiang put a table in front of her door, and placed a cup of "treasure of teas" before each suitor who proposed marriage to her. She spoke, "I will choose my husband today, and I hope God will bless me. I have put my vital energy into the tea. The one in whose cup reveals my figure will be my husband." Hearing this, those who proposed marriage to her all watched the tea in the cups before them. But only in the cup set before the woodcutter, Shi Yong, did the fragrant vapors of the tea curl upward, in the initial form of a green tea leaf unfolding and later turning into a tea tree. People could see Luo Xiang picking tea under the tree, with the girl inside and outside the cup, as well as the tea in the cup and in the mountain, all becoming an integral whole. As a result, Luo Xiang married the woodcutter. Then the news spread to local authorities. The county magistrate duly seized the "treasure of teas" from Luo Xiang and presented it to the imperial court. It was fragrant but no soul could be seen in the teacup. The county magistrate arrested Shi Yong and tortured him. However, Luo Xiang saved his life by reviving him with "treasure of teas" brewed with spring water from Huangshan Mountain.

Another legend about Maofeng tea of Huangshan is also thought-provoking: During the reign of Tianqi in the Ming Dynasty there was a learned, refined, and incorruptible county magistrate named Xiong Kaiyuan. Once he went to the Yungu Temple in the Huangshan Mountain with his pageboy during a spring outing. The elder of the Temple presented him with a kind of fine tea which had sprouts on yellow leaves which looked like white hair. He made tea with the boiling water from a nearby spring, and found that not only did the tea have unparalleled color, fragrance, and taste, but when it changed and rose, the wonder of a white lotus appeared in the air. According to the elder, when the legendary Holy Farmer fell ill after tasting mysterious herbs, the God of Huangshan saved his life with tea. Out of gratitude, the Holy Farmer left them a white lotus seed. Later, a county magistrate who madly desired an official position secretly presented the tea to the Emperor so his meritorious deeds could be recorded. But since he did not know that the white lotus would not appear without the spring water from Huangshan Mountain, he harmed himself in his greed for recognition. Seeing through the corruption of officials, Xiong Kaiyuan resigned and became a monk at the Yungu Temple, accompanied all day by Maofeng tea, spring water, and his fellow monks. Superficially, there seems to be no difference between this story

Huangshan, Anhui Province

and ordinary folktales, but a careful study proves that it is not the case. First, included in it is the story of the Holy Farmer tasting herbs, which repeats the lore that tea was used early in the Holy Farmer's time. Second, the legend that the white lotus would appear if tea was made with the spring water reflects the relationship between Buddhism and tea. Elder Huineng and Xiong Kaiyuan, a Confucian scholar, practiced the tea ceremony together at the Yungu Temple, which demonstrates that a real tea connoisseur must be a detached and virtuous man. As for the county magistrate who was always flattering the Emperor, he had nothing to do with the righteous moral character of Maofeng tea of Huangshan.

Da Hongpao (Red Robe) tea

There are also many legends about the Da Hongpao (Red Robe) tea of Wuyi Mountain. According to some, in a year with poor harvest, an old and kind-hearted woman named Lady Qin saved an old man. In fact, he was one of the immortals, and to show his gratitude he inserted a stick into the earth and the stick became a tea tree. Afterwards, the Emperor dug up the tea tree and planted it in his palace. But the fairylike tea tree rose sharply from the ground and flew to its home on Wuyi Mountain. Its red leaves were like flowing colored clouds, as well as the robe of the tea fairy. Some people, however, say that the Emperor bestowed red robes on three tea trees, for the tea cured the Empress of a disease. It should be noted here that many legends about famous tea include moving love stories about the treatment of disease. This theme stressed the medical value of tea and its pure moral character.

An interesting legend about Junshan tea of Dongting Lake tells of an old Taoist priest who gave advice to the Queen Mother of the State of Chu. The elderly Queen Mother was always falling ill despite the filial devotion of her son, the King. An old Taoist priest with a white beard came to treat her. But he said that nothing was wrong with her except that she ate so many delicacies from land and sea, and, as a result, she was suffering from stomach trouble. Before taking his leave, he left a gourd of divine water, along with the following prescription:

Two decoctions a day, and more vegetables at each meal;
If you want a long life, walk a hundred paces after supper.

The Queen Mother recovered; but a high official of the state wanted to remove the divine water of Junshan Mountain to the royal palace. Angered at this, the old Taoist priest splashed divine water on the side of Junshan Mountain, which in turn became thousands of tea trees as effectual as the divine water. The king of the State of Chu blamed the old Taoist priest for the crime of "deception on the king," but the priest said that if the king had cleaned out all the divine water, he had committed the crime of "deception on the people," for each place had its own way of supporting its own inhabitants. The king had to give in. From then on, he sent a hundred girls in red to pick tea in Junshan Mountain every year. The girls, twenty in each group, were like flowers dotting the rippling green mountain. Seeing the beautiful scenery, the king was in an exalted, poetic mood. "In the vast expanse of green bushes, the girls in red are picking tea leaves." Chanting at this, he suddenly realized that in the Chinese character "tea" (茶) the symbol for "person" is between those for "grass" and "wood," and the original complex form of the stroke "grass" could also be written as a simplified form of the word "twenty," which was the way that the girls were organized into teams.

Chinese character "tea" by Cai Xiang (Song Dynasty)

Why did the king insist on removing the divine spring of the Junshan Mountain, since everything has its own natural relationship? Cleverly contrived, the story satirized and gave advice to the rulers, and brought out the theme in the end with a maxim: After drinking a cup of tea, the king should be sober-minded, not taking too much time and effort to trouble the people.

That good tea is made with good water is the basic requirement of tea as art. On this point the common people are the most qualified to speak, for they often live beside famous waters rather than assiduously seeking their sources. Many stories exist about the discovery and protection of famous springs and waters. For example, the Hupao Spring in Hangzhou is said to have been dug out with superhuman strength by two brothers called Dahu and Erhu, who became tigers in order to save the local people.

In the city of Guilin to the south, with its picturesque karst topography synonymous with China, there is a tale about the White Dragon Spring and Liu Xianyan tea. It is said that the tea made with the water from the White Dragon Spring was fragrant, and out of the vapor flew a white dragon. So the water was treated as a tribute specially paid to the Emperor. The Liu Xianyan tea is said to have been planted by an immortal called Liu Jing in the Song Dynasty. In fact, the so-called immortal was simply a living human being who had attained the Way. We can see from these examples that legends about tea and springs are simply twists on real life.

Some stories reproduce historical facts in a way people love to hear and talk about. Here is the story about an exchange of a horse for *The Book of Tea*: In the last years of the Tang Dynasty, monarchs established separate regimes by force of arms and rebelled against the imperial court. The Emperor was badly in need of horses to put down these rebellions, so the imperial court exchanged tea for horses with the State of Huihe. In the autumn of that year, messengers from both the Tang Dynasty and the State of Huihe met again at the border. This time the messenger from the State of Huihe wanted to exchange a thousand strong horses for *The Book of Tea*. The author of the book, Lu Yu, however, had since

Exchange Tea for Horses Department, Sichuan Province

died, and the book was not yet universally known. So the Emperor ordered his messengers to use all possible means to search for the book in Tiaoxi, Huzhou, where the book was said to have been written, as well as Lu Yu's home county, Jingling (today's Tianmen County in Hubei Province). At last the great poet Pi Rixiu took out a manuscript, which was later exchanged for the horses. From then on *The Book of Tea* was spread abroad. Irrespective of whether the story is derived from the common people or from scholars, it was cleverly invented, for it linked the exchange of tea for horses with the spread of *The Book of Tea*. In fact, the Tang Government kept in frequent contact with the State of Huihe, for it was in the Tang Dynasty that *The Book of Tea* was spread to the northwest part of the Chinese empire.

According to one legend, there is a large camellia in Luliang County, Yunnan Province. It was more than 20 feet (6.6 meters) tall and one arm span in diameter, and each of its flowers had nine stamens and eighteen petals. People called it the King of Camellias. The legend about the tree, however, is linked with the history of Wu Sangui's governing of Yunnan. It is said that because Wu Sangui plotted to be Emperor after having dominated Yunnan, he built a palace in the Wuhua Mountain and the Axiang Garden by the Lotus Pool, and searched everywhere for exotic flowers and rare herbs. Then he forced the transplantation of King of Camellias in Luliang County to his palace. It turned out that the tree had an iron will, growing leaves but not coming into flower, in spite of scars of the wounds inflicted on it by Wu Sangui's whip. Three years later, Wu Sangui wanted to kill the gardener in a fury. Then the tea fairy came into his dream, singing:

111

"Don't be drunk, San gui. The gardener is innocent, but you are mistaken.
As a girl from a peasant family, I don't seek wealth and rank.
I only wish to go home
And spend the rest of my life."

Hearing this, Wu Sangui wielded his sword, but instead of killing the tea fairy, he cut off the dragon's head on a nearby chair. Then he heard the tea fairy singing:

"Mean, low and notorious,
You have betrayed your master for glory.
You disreputable gang is completely absorbed in
Building your palace,
With your throne stained with blood.
Since what you did has caused
Widespread indignation and discontent,
Ghosts will haunt you and punish you."

🍵 *Wu Sangui*

Hearing this, Wu Sangui was dizzy, and broke out in a cold sweat all over from fear. Suddenly he woke up and found that he was having a dream. Fearing of the haunting of ghosts, his adviser suggested that he "relegate" the King of Camellias back to Luliang County. This story mainly illustrates the inflexible character of tea by cleverly quoting the historical fact that Wu Sangui rose in rebellion and declared himself Emperor. Actually, there are many such historical stories in Yunnan. For example, many stories tell of Zhuge Liang, who taught people how to plant and use tea, directly stressing the blending of foreign culture with Chinese culture. Zhuge Liang was also known as Kong Ming, so in many places in Yunnan Province, people call some big tea trees "Kong Ming Trees." We do not know whether people in Yunnan learned to plant and use tea only after Kong Ming reached Yunnan. But spiritually, people of different nationalities value historical figures for different reasons.

Some stories, whether made up by scholars or by common people, are particularly interesting, such as the story about "serving tea according to loneliness and nobleness:"

112 Zheng Banqiao always pursued his studies in Zhenjiang. One day he went to the abbot's room in the Jinshan Temple to enjoy calligraphy. At first, the snobbish abbot did not even glance at Zheng Banqiao, who was dressed in plain clothes. He reluctantly told Zheng to sit down. Then he said to the little monk attending, "Tea!" During their talk, the abbot learned that Zheng and he were from the same town, so he said, "Please sit down!" Then he cried to the little

🍵 Calligraphy and painting by Zheng Banqiao (Qing Dynasty)

monk, "Serve tea!" But when he learned that the visitor was the well-known Zheng Banqiao, he was so delighted that he said quickly, "Please take the seat of honor!" And he hurriedly ordered the little monk, "Serve fragrant tea!"

Having drunk tea, Zheng stood up and was about to take his leave. Then the old monk asked Zheng to bestow on him some couplets or treasured scrolls of calligraphy or paintings.

Zheng waved his hand and wrote the first line, "Sit down, please sit down, please take the seat of honor!" And the second line was, "Tea, serve tea, serve fragrant tea!"

Another story tells of Zhu Yuanzhang, the founder of the Ming Dynasty, who bestowed a cap and belt on a waiter in a teahouse. Once, Zhu Yuanzhang was inspecting an academy of learning after an evening banquet. A cook there presented him with a cup of scented tea. It happened that Zhu was thirsty at the time. The more he drank the tea, the more he enjoyed its fragrance. On impulse, he granted the cook a cap and belt on a sudden impulse. Unimpressed by this, however, a student in the yard sang loudly, "Ten years of studies in spite of hardships is no match for a small cup of tea." All were surprised at the student's offense to the Emperor. But Zhu said the second line with a smile: "He has less knowledge than you, but you have a worse fate than he." The story showed Zhu's liking for tea. Also, it is consistent with history. Being of low origin, Zhu was considerate of laborers. And since he almost had no schooling, he laid stress only on practice to the neglect of knowledge.

113

🌸 *Chou Yin: Brewing Tea and Talking About Painting (Ming Dynasty)*

Chapter 7

7. Folk Traditions and Marriage Customs

Folk customs are an important part of national culture. In the past, and even today, folk customs in China have their own distinctive local features. It is said: "Only ten *li* apart, but the customs are quite different." Customs were colorful and varied in attitude, a fact which is often ignored. However, they reflect profound cultural psychologies. The same is true of tea-drinking. Although popular drinking methods were not as standardized as the Confucian, Taoist and Buddhist tea culture systems, most of the common people carried out the spirit of tea culture in their work, clothing, food, shelter and transportation, and various social rites such as weddings and funerals, and social interaction, showing that the spirit of Chinese tea culture was integrated with the thoughts of the common people.

It was a popular Chinese custom to entertain one's guest with tea to show great respect. People in different areas had various ways of serving tea.

Entertain one's guest with tea

Wealthy and influential families north of the Yellow River served their guests with three separate "rounds" of tea. The host first led the guest to the central room. After greeting each other, the host would ask their servants or children to serve tea. The first round, which was presented when the guest had just arrived, was served only as a formality, and it was not impolite for the guest to leave it untouched if he or she so desired. The second course was served as host and guest talked with each other. The guest tasted the wonderful tea carefully. They talked while drinking. The third course was served after they had finished talking, and the tea had become weak. The guest then took his leave, and the host saw him off. However, close friends did not adhere to these formalities when they wanted to talk to their hearts' content.

People in regions south of the Yangtze River have entertained guests with the best tea and food to give blessing and show respect to them since the Song and Yuan dynasties. Hunan people, for example, entertained guests with tea containing fried soy beans, sesame, and ginger slices. Besides drinking the tea, the guests chewed beans, sesame, and tea leaves. Villagers in Hubei Province drank plain water during ordinary times, and entertained guests with tea made of puffed rice and malt, or offered their guests *yuanbao* tea during the Spring Festival to wish them luck and bring wealth and happiness in the coming year. Such tea was made of Chinese olives or kumquats which had been cut open, and looked like *yuanbao* (a characteristically-shaped gold ingot).

Besides entertaining guests with tea, people presented it as a gift to their relatives or friends. During the Song Dynasty, people in the capital city of Kaifeng were very righteous and warm-hearted. When a resident moved into a new house, the neighbors offered him tea, or invited him to go to their homes to drink tea to show their friendliness. Such tea was called *zhicha*. When the capital of the Southern Song Dynasty later moved to Hangzhou, this tradi-

🍵 *People presented tea as a gift to relatives or friends*

tion was continued in that region. The custom of showing one's friendliness and respect to a guest by offering tea has been preserved up to the present. Every family in Hangzhou presented fresh tea and ripe fruit as gifts to their relatives and friends at the beginning of summer. This custom, called *qijiacha,* was handed down from the Song Dynasty, and recorded in a book written during the Ming Dynasty. According to the *Records of Chinese Customs,* people of the State of Wu sought tea from their neighbors, and brewed it with the previous year's charcoal at the start of summer.

Tea was used not only to serve guests, but also to show mutual respect and affection among family members, and the feudal order of importance or seniority in human relationships. As far back as the Song and Yuan dynasties, it was an important component of family rites to serve tea to the family elders. The Chinese stressed the genetic connection, family relationships, and advocated respect for aged people and protection of the young. In old China, children of a wealthy and influential family gave morning greetings to their parents, and the oldest son or daughter served them a cup of newly brewed scented tea on behalf of the other children. The custom was more popular in South China. A bride had to get up early and serve newly brewed scented tea to her in-laws when she greeted them on the second morning after the wedding. The rite was designed to show three things: the bride's filial respect, keeping early hours, and being industrious and thrifty in running her home. In the land of tea, a young married woman who could not brew and serve tea in this fashion was regarded as clumsy and unreasonable.

🍵 *Tea vat*

Well-off families in Jiangxi Province followed a fixed rule when drinking tea. Servants, long-term hired hands and sedan-chair bearers drank tea from *baohu,* a huge tin teapot covered with cotton and placed in a large vat. They tipped it to pour out the tea through a little hole in the vat. Ordinary family members and guests drank tea from *tenghu,* a smaller china pot in a cane container. The master of the house or distinguished guests coming on festival days were served newly brewed tea in teacups with covers. This procedure reflected the obsession with hierarchical relationships and respect for seniority.

The ethnic Han Chinese tea rite was spread to other Chinese ethnic minorities. In the Dali Area where the Bai ethnic group lived, each family drank tea while admiring the beauty of flowers at every festival and at New Year. They built small gardens, or grew trees and flowers or potted plants in the courtyards or on the steps. They sometimes invited their friends to brew tea while admiring the beauty of flowers. A child had to learn to serve tea to their parents or guests. The first test for a bride was to see whether she could rise early, and serve tea to her parents-in-law before they got up to show her filial respect for them. It was the main spirit of the Chinese family tea rite to show respect for one's elders by serving them tea. Although the family tea rite in feudal societies contained some negative factors such as the view that men were superior to women, it advocated that people should respect the old and cherish the young, live with each other in harmony, and be industrious and thrifty in running their homes.

119

The tea rite was most widely reflected in wedding customs. Compared with Westerners, the Chinese attached even greater importance to family connections, and regarded marriage as the most important event of their lives. Tea represented purity, firmness, and the view that the more children one had, the happier one would be. The Chinese regarded tea as the purest aesthetic essence, symbolizing pure and noble love between man and woman on the occasion of marriage. The ancients believed that transplanted tea could not survive (however, people have now mastered the skill), so tea was sometimes called *buqian* (unmovable) to express unswerving love. As tea had many seeds, it symbolized the Chinese view that the more children and grandchildren one had, the happier one would be. So, when combined with marriage systems, the tea rite became one of the most important rites of one's life.

Wedding customs

Tea and Chinese Culture

In South China among the Han people, upon an engagement, the bridegroom-to-be offered betrothal gifts to the bride's family, an action which was called *xiachali* (offering tea). The wedding custom was called *sanchali* (three tea rites) in regions south of the Yangtze River. It can be defined in two ways: It may refer to three courtesies on the engagement and wedding ceremony of a new couple: that is, *xiachali* on the engagement, *dingchali* on the wedding ceremony, and *hechali* on the wedding night. It may, however, refer to the three tea courses of the wedding ceremony: the first course, ginkgo; the second, lotus seeds and dates; and the third, tea. In both cases, tea symbolized pure and unswerving love.

Tea was first used in weddings as far back as the Song Dynasty. The bridegroom presented tea as a betrothal gift to the bride's family when he made an offer of marriage, which was called "knocking at the door." The matchmaker was also called "the person carrying tea caddies." On the day before the marriage, the bride's family went to the bridegroom's house

🍵 *Drama: The Peach Blossom Fan*

to decorate the bridal curtain and chamber, and to offer them tea and wine. In the famous work of literature, *The Peach Blossom Fan* written by Kong Shangren, it states: "The bridal sedan chair was ready to carry the bride to the bridegroom's house, and the bridegroom's family has offered adequate tea as a betrothal gift." Quotations such as these show that tea was a time-honored symbol of marriage. Tea was essential to the old wedding customs in Jiangsu Province. The matchmaker passed the card containing the hour, date, month and year of the bride's birth written in red golden paint, and the bridegroom's side offered tea, fruits, silver, and gold as betrothal gifts. On the wedding day, the bridegroom rode on horseback to the bride's home with a sedan chair retinue following, and waited at the gate. He had to make a bow with his hands folded in front of him whenever he entered a door until he reached the central room, and greeted his father-in-law and the honored guests. After he was served three courses of tea, he went to his mother-in-law's room to wait for the bride to enter the sedan chair. This was called "tea served when opening the door."

Tea occupied an important place in wedding ceremonies in Hunan and Jiangxi provinces, known as famous tea production areas. A popular local saying goes: "young men and women would pledge to marry by drinking tea together." If the young man and woman agreed to meet each other, the matchmaker would lead the young man to the girl's home on a fixed day. If the girl agreed to associate with him, she would serve him a cup of tea. If the man was satisfied, he would leave payment for tea in the cup; otherwise he would also drink tea to show his respect to the young

Tea occupied an important place in life

woman, then place the cup on the table upside down. The payment for tea should be even in number, ranging from two to 100 *yuan*. If the man drank the tea, the marriage would have hope of success. Young men and women in Hunan Province showed their reactions to each other by drinking tea and eating stewed eggs. If the girl went to the man's home, and the man was satisfied with her, he would offer her three or more eggs; if he was not, he offered only two eggs. The girl would show her good faith by eating the three or more eggs happily. If the man went to the girl's home, and the girl was satisfied with him, she would offer him tea and eggs; if not, only tea.

The tea rite concerning engagement ceremonies in Hunan Province was unique in style. The bridegroom's side went to the bride's home to offer betrothal gifts including *yanchapan*—a plate on which were displayed patterns such as "the man and the phoenix," and "the magpie carrying a plum branch in its bill." The patterns were made of dyed lampwicks, and the space between filled with tea and salt. The custom was called *zhengcha* (formal tea). If the bride's

121

family accepted it, the marriage would be settled, and both of them could never go back on their word.

In Hunan Province, the bridegroom and bride would meet their elders and offer them scented tea when guests took their seats after the wedding ceremony. Each elder member of the family would put a red paper envelope containing money on the tea tray after he or she drank tea. In some areas, the bridegroom and bride drank tea together on the wedding night, just as newly married couples in North China drank "cross-cupped wine" from one another's cups. When the bride entered the bridal chamber, the bridegroom offered the bride a cup of tea with both hands. The bride took a sip, and the bridegroom followed. Thus they completed the most solemn ceremony in their lives.

Brides of many ethnic groups are found in China

It was a popular Chinese custom to celebrate weddings in the bridal chamber. People in Hunan Province held such celebrations centered around tea, such as *hehecha* and *chitaicha*. *Hehecha* was recorded in the *Records of Chinese Customs,* and it is still popular in many places. The bridegroom and bride sat on the same bench, facing each other, and putting their left legs on the other's right legs. The bridegroom put his left hand on the bride's shoulder, and the bride put her right hand on the bridegroom's shoulder. Then they closed their thumbs and index fingers of their free hands to form a square. They held a cup filled with tea in the "square," then people drank tea from it in turn. *Taicha* was another custom. The newly married couple carried a tea tray on which were placed cups filled with tea, and asked guests to drink tea in turn. Every guest should speak words of praise before they drank tea; if he could not think of praise, he had to give up his turn to the next guest. In some areas, the newly married couples offered both tea and eggs to their elders, who then gave them red paper envelope containing money as a gift.

The tea rite of weddings in Huzhou, Zhejiang Province, was similar to that of Hunan and

122

Jiangxi provinces. The acceptance of the betrothal presents offered by the bridegroom's side was called *chicha* (drinking tea) or *shoucha* (accepting tea); the newly married couple offered tea to show respect to their seniors. The gifts given by the seniors were called *chabao*. In North China, the bride returned to her mother's home on the third day of the wedding, which was called *huimen,* while in some areas of Zhejiang Province, the bride's parents went to see their daughter on the third day, which was called *wangzhao*. The parents would bring dry beans, sesame, and tea gathered before the Grain Rain, the 6th solar term, to the bridegroom's home to make tea. The two families talked while drinking, which was called *qingjiapocha* (tea offered by the bride's mother).

Once the couple had borne children tea played a different role. In Huzhou, a baby had its head shaved on the completion of its first month of life, and its head was washed with tea to wish it intelligence, and to bring it a long life of abundance and respect. The custom was called *chayukaishi*.

123

The Bai ethnic group in Dali County, Yunnan Province, lived at the foot of Mount Cangshan by Erhai Lake, the birthplace of tea. The spirit of tea was reflected in the area's

🍵 *Bai ethnic group in Yunnan*

wedding customs. Young girls were skillful in baking tea leaves. They stewed water on an iron tripod mounted in the central room, and baked tea in a small sand jar by its side. Then they poured boiling water on the baked tea when it sent out an enchanting fragrance. Foam rose from the mouth of the jar like rounded pincushions. One of the standards by which the bride was appraised was whether she could offer such wonderful baked tea to her parents-in-law. The bridegroom's friends celebrated the wedding in the bridal chamber, and the newly married couple offered them three courses of tea, which was different from that served at ordinary times. The first course was bitter tea; the second, sweet tea with brown sugar and nuts; and the third, milk tea made with brown sugar. "The first course was bitter; the second, sweet; and the third would lead a person to endless aftertastes." Such was the philosophy of life in these folk customs.

In Menghai County, Yunnan Province, there was a local custom that the bride would climb a tree to gather tea. The local people believed that the higher she climbed, and the more tea she gathered, the luckier the couple would be. The bridegroom might feel embarrassed to tell a stranger the reason for the custom, but if questioned closely over and over again, he would finally state: "We gathered tea so that it would bless us to have a lasting affection towards each other, exuberant vitality, and many children."

The Lahu ethnic group living by the Lancangjiang River enjoyed freedom of marriage. When a couple

🍃 *2,700-year-old tea trees (Yunnan Province)*

were attracted to each other, they would pledge to marry, and finally tell their parents. The bridegroom's family asked a matchmaker to go to the bride's home to make an offer of marriage. The matchmaker presented a pair of candles, cigarettes, tea and other things as betrothal gifts on behalf of the bridegroom, among which tea was an essential item. The Lahu people believed that if the bridegroom did not offer tea, the marriage would not be legitimate. After the formal wedding ceremony, the bride and bridegroom carried water and offered it to their parents and the matchmaker. Such a marriage would be regarded as a happy and auspicious one.

🍵 Wedding ceremony of the Lahu ethnic group

125

Tea also had an important place in the wedding ceremony of the Maonan ethnic group in the northwest of Guangxi Province. On the wedding day, after the man sent by the bridegroom's side had lunch at the bride's home, the bride's family started to "fold the quilt." The bride's mother filled a large copper pan with red eggs, glutinous rice, wicker, tangerines, melon seeds, copper coins, and tea—always an essential item. The bride's sisters, aunts, and female in-laws folded the quilt into a square, and placed it on a yoke called a *gang*, with a copper pan on one end, and a tin teapot on the other, and draped it with many cloth shoes made by the bride. The practice of "transforming marriage" was popular in the Maonan ethnic group. When an elder brother died, the younger one would marry his wife, or vice versa. The ceremony was called "transforming tea."

In the Achang ethnic group, the matchmaker went to the bride's home to offer two bags of tea, tobacco, and sugar. On the third day of the wedding, when the bride's family went to the bridegroom's home to send her dowry, the bridegroom's family proposed a toast: "Please ride the large white horse;" together with another toast on departure: "Please ride the large red horse to return home!"

After being planted, it will take at least four years for a tea tree to produce tea of harvest quality.

The wedding custom of the Qiang ethnic group in the Aba area of Sichuan Province was very interesting. As a special local product, tea was an essential wedding gift. On the wedding day, three-gun salute was fired whenever the contingents of people who go to the bride's home to escort her to the wedding passed a village. Villagers went out to see the fun. The relatives of the bridegroom and the bride entertained the contingent with tea and food made of corn, highland barley, wheat, and soy beans. They moved on after drinking and eating. In this way, they showed their blessings and friendship. Finally, the bride reached the bridegroom's home.

Besides showing faithfulness and respect, ethnic groups in the northwest of China showed their wealth through the tea rite at weddings. Tea was essential in their daily life, but was hard to come by. In the Sala ethnic group in Qinghai, the bridegroom's side asked the matchmaker to go to the bride's home on an auspicious day to offer a pair of earrings and a package of *fucha* tea as "engagement tea;" a custom called *xiding*. In the Bonan ethnic group in Gansu Province, the bridegroom's father or uncle, together with the matchmaker, went to the bride's home to offer a pair of earrings, two packages of *fucha* tea, and some clothes. The Yugu ethnic group valued tea highly. A lump of *fucha* tea could be exchanged for two sheep. The bridegroom had to offer a horse, an ox, more than ten sheep, 20 pieces of cloth, and two lumps of *fucha* tea to the bride's family.

Matchmaking was called *shuocha* in the Hui ethnic group. Parents of both sides took a look at their prospective daughter-in-law or son-in-law on such a meeting. If the bridegroom's parents took a fancy to the bride, the matchmaker would go to her home to bring back words and offer *fucha* tea. If the bride's side agreed, they would accept the tea. Thus they were engaged to each other. The rite was called *dingcha* (betrothal tea) or *xicha* (wedding tea). The bride's family divided the tea into small pieces, and gave it to their relatives, friends, and neighbors as gifts.

Tea also had an important place in Tibetan wedding custom. Young men and women measured their future husband or wife by his or her appearance and moral outlook instead of financial situation and betrothal gifts. They sang songs when they pledged to marry, using tea as a metaphor for love:

🔹 *Tibetans making milky tea*

Could we eat zanba in our bags together?

Could we brew tea in our pots together?

Could we exchange our golden bracelets and silver rings?

Could we exchange our long and short belts?

From this pledge, we can see that Tibetans regarded tea as important as golden bracelets and silver belts. Buttered tea was also essential for a wedding.

The Manchu ethnic group developed from the Nüzhen ethnic group in China's far northeast. The Nüzhen ethnic group founded the Jin Dynasty (1115-1234) and still preserved the remnants of a matriarchal system. Tea was used in their wedding ceremonies, and a man's proposal was called *xiachali* (offering tea). On the wedding day, the bride's family sat on a *kang* (a raised heated platform used for sleeping) to receive the bridegroom's family. Then they drank tea and ate candied fruits together. In the Qing Dynasty, the Manchus continued this old custom. They also called an engagement *xiachali*, although it was a simplified form of the earlier custom.

Tea was widely used in weddings of many Chinese ethnic groups. It had an important place in wedding customs in the central plains and border areas, southwest, northwest and northeast China. It showed that people everywhere believed that tea was the symbol of firmness, purity, love, and luck.

In addition to weddings, tea has been used in funerals and sacrificial rites. According to a story in *The Book of Tea* quoted from *Strange Tales* (a collection of stories from the pre-Qin period written by Liu Jingshu in the State of Song during the Southern dynasties), Chen Wu's widow lived with two sons when she was still young. The family loved sampling tea, and often presented tea as a sacrificial offering to a ghost, for there was an old tomb near their home. The sons wanted to remove the tomb, and Chen Wu's widow tried hard to persuade them to give up the idea. At night, she dreamt that the ghost came to thank her: "I have lived here for more than 300 years. Your two sons wanted to destroy the tomb. Fortunately, you protected me, and often offered me excellent tea. I will pay you a debt of gratitude!" They found 100,000 coins the next day. This story is one of the earliest records of using tea as a sacrificial offering.

Archaeological discoveries have proved the custom of using tea as a funerary object. For example, a box of tea was found in the famous Tombs of the Han Dynasty at Mawangdui in Changsha City, Hunan Province. The murals in the Tombs of the Liao Dynasty (907-1125) in Xuanhua City, Hebei Province, vividly depict the scene of making and drinking tea. The Chinese regarded death as the end of their mortal lives, and wished to continue their lives after they died. They believed that they could be reborn after death, although they contradicted themselves by also imagining life in the underworld. Therefore, tea became a funerary object so that people could continue drinking in the after-life.

However, there were many far-fetched superstitious stories about popular funeral customs.

It was widely believed in China that ghosts in the netherworld would compel a person who had just died to drink a magic potion to make him forget all the past on earth, or lead him into a maze so that the ghosts could humiliate and enslave him. The Chinese believed that one should be reasonable and sober, and it was unwise to drink the magic potion. Tea could help people keep a clear head. So tea became an important component part of funeral customs in many tea producing areas. According to the *Records of Chinese Customs,* people in Zhejiang Province and some other areas believed that "besides a silver ingot, the family of the deceased should put a ball made of mannan leaves in his mouth, and a pack of tea in his hand so that he could not be filled with the magic potion. They would mutter Buddhist scriptures when they carried the coffin. This custom was also popular in Anhui Province. It was not only applied to the dead, but also to the living. Necromancy was popular in Jiangsu Province. When a child was ill, a man held his clothes on a scale, and another man carried a lantern. They echoed each other's utterances, and sprinkled rice and tea while walking so that ghosts could not entice the child's lost soul. The ceremony was called "calling home the lost soul."

Tea was rare in North China, so it was not often used in funerals. However, it was widely used in sacrificial rites to ghosts, spirits, and ancestors. It is interesting to note that the Chinese believed that everything had a spirit so there were mountain gods, water gods, town gods, local gods of the land, tree gods, grain gods, flower gods, and insect gods. The Door God and Kitchen God were regarded as the most important gods of the family. The Door God, trans-

The murals in the Tombs of the Liao Dynasty (907-1125) in Xuanhua City, Hebei Province

129

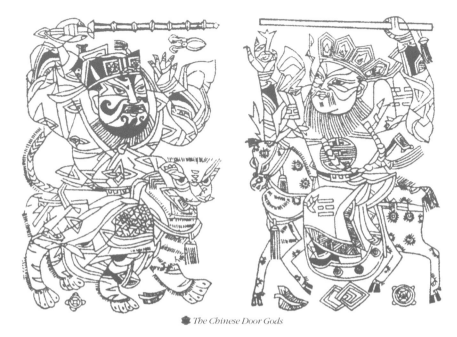

🍵 *The Chinese Door Gods*

formed from a hero in history, blessed and protected peaceful family life. It is said that a sacrificial rite to the Kitchen God was held throughout China on the 23rd of the twelfth month of the lunar year in commemoration of the date when he went up to the sky. But Chinese custom also treats gods in peculiar ways sometimes. For example, people made fun of the Kitchen God. On the 23rd of the twelfth month of the lunar year, each family tried to bribe him with *zaotang*, which was called *tanggua* (candied melons) in North China, so that he would not secretly inform on them in heaven. In the Liaoyang area of northeast China, every family fashioned a horse made with *gaoliang* (sorghum) shafts so that the Kitchen God could ride it to go up to heaven. At night, they offered a cup of tea. Some people held that the tea was given to the horse, while others insisted that it was prepared for the Kitchen God.

🍵 *Kitchen God animation on internet*

Chapter 8

8. *The Art of Serving Tea*

Huzhou Prefecture, Zhejiang Province, is an old and highly revered tea growing region in China. It is the place where Lu Yu wrote *The Book of Tea.* In the ranges of green mountains with their clear streams, lakes, and rivers, the rich soil here is ideal for growing tea. More importantly, many different forms of ancient tea art, which can be called typical tea ceremonial practices among the common people, have been preserved intact and survive and continue to thrive today.

Nowadays, the Huzhou people are particular about the procedures of making tea, which mainly include welcoming their guests, setting tea sets on the table, boiling water, pouring boiling water into the teapot, stirring the tea in teacups, serving tea, tasting tea, etc. Before guests arrive, the host makes the preparations, such as preparing fine tea, condiments, fruit, clean tea sets, clear water, and dried bamboo splints. When the guests enter, the host lets them sit in the seat of honor. The host hangs up a special pot for boiling water, which can be treated as a variant of Lu Yu's "tea boiler," and uses the thin bamboo splints as fuel for the fire. When the water boils, the host takes out small bags of tender tea leaves and pours them into the bowl pinch by pinch. Then the host grasps a handful of dry, pickled and cooked green soybeans and grips other condiments on the table with chopsticks, and then puts them into the bowl. At this time the host pours the boiling water in the pot into the bowl about of the way to the top, while stirring the tea and water with chopsticks. Drinking tea in this way is a

🍵 *The Tomb of Lu Yu , Huzhou Prefecture, Zhejiang Province*

custom handed down from the Tang Dynasty.

At the moment when the flavors of tea and condiments are mingled in the water, a fragrant smell strikes the nose. It is the best time to drink. So, the host holds the cups of tea before the guests respectfully and skillfully, saying, "Please drink tea." The host then takes out nuts and melon seeds, and puts them on the center of the table. After that, the host and the guests drink and eat as they talk. The tea made with dried green soybeans is salty. Generally speaking, the tea, condiments, and green soybeans are eaten together after the boiling water has been added to the tea three times, after which point the host makes a fresh pot.

This type of tea drinking is like art and resembled a beautiful poem in how it is composed and executed. In Huzhou Prefecture, no respect for guests can be shown without serving tea in this fashion.

Taking a panoramic view of the tea ceremony of Huzhou Prefecture, we can see that there are many similarities between the tea ceremony of contemporary Huzhou and that of ancient China:

1. The tea as art form has certain rules, the first of which is to create the atmosphere of drinking tea through graceful manipulation.

2. The ancient custom of adding condiments to tea is preserved.

3. Unlike the way of drinking tea in north China, in which tea is poured into cups from a big teapot, tea is made in individual teacups.

4. After boiling water is poured on the tea, the tea must be stirred vigorously. This is similar to the common tea ceremonies of the Yuan and Ming dynasties.

5. The tea ceremony emphasizes more respect for guests than the quenching of thirst.

6. The ancient tea party is preserved, with the tea party of Huzhou being a typical tea ceremony of the common people.

7. Unlike ancient hermits, or those recluses who derive inner satisfaction from drinking tea, most Chinese people love tea the way they love life, and the social interaction tea provides is best exemplified by the tea ceremony.

There are different opinions about the name of Congou, or Kong Fu tea. Some people think that it is called thus because it takes a lot of time to process the tea leaves; some think that it derives its name because it takes a long time to taste mouthful by mouthful this strong and bitter tea contained in tiny teacups; and some think that it is so called because it stresses the method of tasting and needs special operating skills. All these opinions seem reasonable, but the third one is the most rational.

Kong Fu tea is popular in Fujian and Guangdong provinces and other places southeast of China. For example, the Chaozhou and Shantou Kong Fu tea has an integrated ceremony encompassing the reflected spirit, the etiquette, the skills of both making tea and pouring tea for guests, and the appraisal of the quality of the tea.

Generally speaking, there are altogether four people, including the host or hostess, in a Chaozhou and Shantou Kong Fu tea ceremony. This limitation of the number of the people is similar to the ideas of the tea drinkers of the Ming and Qing dynasties, who thought that tea drinking should take place in an intimate setting among those with kindred intellect and appreciation.

 Kong Fu tea is popular in Fujian and Guangdong Provinces

Starting from the host's right side the guests sit on both sides of the table according to their generation or status, just like the feudal order of importance or seniority in China's ancient religious communities and temples.

After the guests sit at the table, the host or hostess begins to operate in strict accordance with the old tea rules, in particular concerning tea sets, water quality, tea leaves, and the ways of making and drinking tea.

The tea set includes the teapot, teacups, and the utensils for containing tea dregs. The teapot itself is tiny, almost miniature, and no larger than a persimmon. The ceramic

 The teapot is no larger than a persimmon

137

teacups have very thin walls. The ceramic utensil for containing tea dregs, like a drum, is composed of a plate, which resembles the surface of a drum. The plate has small holes, through which the tea to rinse teacups at the beginning of the ceremony can flow into. Boiling water poured on the lid of the teapot to keep the inside tea warm also falls out of the way through the holes. The utensil for containing tea dregs also holds the remaining water and tea. The Kong Fu tea ceremony is very particular about the quality of the teapot. After the Ming and Qing dynasties, teapots made from *zisha* were used because of the idea that tea art should return to its original nature, but the teapot used in the Chaozhou and Shantou Kong Fu tea ceremony is made from the soft earth of Chaozhou, for this kind of teapot absorbs the fragrance of tea more easily. In this regard, different teapots are used for different types of tea. For example, scented tea needs porcelain teapots to keep its fragrance; it is better to use china teapots or even glass, rather than sand, or clay-based pots, to hold weak green tea so as to keep the fragrance of the tea and observe the shape and color of the tea leaves. Red tea (black tea) or semi-fermented oolong tea needs sand or clay-based tea pots, which give an impression of primitive simplicity and can easily send forth the fragrance of the tea. Before a new teapot is formally used, it must first be soaked in freshly-made tea water for over three months to keep the teapot fragrant throughout. Teapots made of Chaozhou earth contain their own unique fragrance. The teacups are exquisitely small like walnuts or apricots, but are simple and strong.

Tea and Chinese Culture

In *Classified Collection of Writings on Various Subjects of the Qing Dynasty,* a sketchbook written by Xu Ke, there is an interesting story which demonstrates the importance of soaking the teapot with tea water before it is first used. It was said that a rich man of Chaozhou liked tea very much. One day, a beggar came to his door. Leaning against the door, the beggar begged for tea instead of food, saying, "I hear you have the nicest tea. Could you give me a pot of it?" The rich man felt it ridiculous to hear this. He said, "Could it be said that you, a beggar, have an idea of tea?" The beggar said, "I too was once rich. But as I indulged in tea all day I squandered my wealth. Now I have to make a living by begging to support my family." Hearing this, the rich man readily gave him a cup of quality Kong Fu tea, for he thought that he had met a kindred spirit. After tasting the tea, the beggar said, "Sure enough, you made nice tea, but it is not mellow enough, for you used a new teapot." Then the beggar took out an old light-colored teapot out of his sleeves. When the pot lid was opened, a wondrous fragrance immediately struck the rich man's nose. The beggar said that though he was penniless and often suffered from cold and hunger, he always held the teapot close. The rich man liked the teapot so much that he wanted to pay 3,000 taels of gold for it. But the beggar hated to part with it. He said, "I want only half of the money you offered, but could we not share the teapot?" The rich man gladly accepted, and from then on they became close friends.

🍵 *Tea leaves comprise 70 percent of the volume of the teapot*

Making tea demands both patience and dexterity. The tea leaves may account for 70 percent of the volume of the teapot, so that they extend to the top of the teapot after steeping. The tea made the first time is used for washing cups rather than drinking, creating the proper atmosphere of tea in every regard. The host then pours boiling water into the teapot. This time the tea leaves are exposed and immediately send forth their fragrance. The host begins to offer tea to the guests, placing four small cups in a circle, and then

shuttles among them with the small teapot until each cup is filled 70 percent of its volume with tea. At this time the tea made for the second time is precisely used up. This way of serving tea is called "Lord Guan Patrolling the City." The rest of the tea is poured into the four cups little by little, a technique called "Marquis Han Xin Mustering His Troops." The four cups put together implies the gathering of host and guests.

139

"Lord Guan Patrolling the City" shows not only superior skills but also complete success according to Chinese philosophy, and "Marquis Han Xin Mustering His Troops" indicates the great harmony reflected in the sharing of the essence of tea.

The host then holds the small cups of tea before the guests. First, the guest of honor are served, and then the other guests according to their generation and age. Finally the host joins them. There are special skills of tasting this kind of tea. Instead of drinking the tea in one mouthful, you should let it turn around your tongue and fully realize its fragrance before you swallow it. Then you must show the bottom of the teacup to the host as you drink to express your sincere gratitude as well as your praise for their superior tea making skills.

🍵 *Smell and fully realize the fragrance of tea before you taste*

In this way several rounds of tea can be enjoyed, all the while the host and the guest enjoy the fragrance and aroma of the tea blending amid their conversations. At the last round of drinking, the host takes the tea leaves out of the teapot with a bamboo clip and puts them in a tiny cup to let the guests enjoy the beautiful natural tea leaves and at the same time to show them that the used tea leaves will not be re-steeped again. This kind of Kong Fu tea is not made only by the rich. Small workshops and stalls in Chaozhou and Shantou sell it by the roadside. Even farmers there who carry produce down the mountains pull out teasets, heat up water and make tea in the mountains when they take a rest. And it is routine for them to make this kind of tea when they are at home. At hotels and restaurants in modern cities and towns,

Kong Fu tea is also made at counters to receive guests. Kong Fu tea demands particular water requirements. Mountain farmers are not very rich, but still quite a few old people of Chaozhou and Shantou buy mountain spring water to make tea. People of Chaozhou and Shantou are tightly bound to the simple teasets, which are robust and long lasting. Once drinking this kind of tea, farmers toiling at work all day will feel as if fragrance has arisen from below their tongues, and feel tired no longer.

Yunnan Province possesses both the human environment and the natural environment fit for planting tea, and it is said to have "the best in the world." The "nine-procedure" tea and the "three-taste" tea are representative of the Yunnan tea culture.

Since Lu Yu wrote *The Book of Tea,* the Chinese people have advocated telling stories about tea and enjoying the sight of tea paintings as they drink. The nine-procedure tea means the nine procedures of tea as art, i.e., appraising tea, washing teasets, putting tea leaves into the teapot, pouring hot water into the teapot, stirring the tea, pouring the tea into teacups, offering tea to the guests, and drinking tea together. These jobs are often done by Yunnan girls, who are beautiful and graceful by nature. Upon prompting by their parents, the may set out some rare teas for the guests to appraise and choose. This choice is determined by the natural conditions of Yunnan Province, for in other parts of China, it is not easy to get even one kind of fine tea, to say nothing of selecting one kind from many. After the guests finish selecting their tea, the girl washes clean the wax-printed tea cloth and all sorts of teasets, puts tea leaves into the teapot, pours hot water into it, and then stirs the tea. When the sweet smell of the tea floats in the air and the color of the tea is just right, the girl pours the tea into the teacups adeptly and gracefully, and presents the cups one after another to the guests according to the order of their age, generation, or status. When the host says "Have a cup of tea, please," the guests may drink the tea. After several rounds of drinks, the host will tell some stories or legends about tea, and talk about the beautiful scenery of Yunnan Province. The beauty of the home province of tea, as well as the friendship of the host, is reflected through the nine-procedure tea.

141

Oolong tea contains a large quantity of polyphenols, which can emulsify fats in the digestive tract.

Chapter 9

9. Tea in China's Hinterland

The spiritual sense of tea is stressed by all ethnic groups of China, a rare occurrence in world dietary history.

The ethnic groups of southwest China live in compact communities in Yunnan, Guizhou, and Sichuan provinces. As original tea-growing areas, these places are rich in tea culture. In particular, when the traditional tea culture fell into decay in modern times in the central plains (comprising the middle and lower reaches of the Yellow River), many tea ceremonies and customs survived in the southwest because the simple folkways and the fact that local culture was deeply entrenched and less severely affected by outside forces or other historical events.

According to historical information, ethnic groups of southwest China knew much about tea, and both used and planted tea earlier than those ethnic groups of the Central Plains.

This can be proved by the story about Yao Bai, who planted tea and distributed land among the Jinuos of Yunnan Province. Long ago, there lived an ancestress of the Jinuos, whose name was Yao Bai. She not only created heaven and earth, but also decided to distribute land to the ethnic groups. The Jinuos, however, failed to attend the meeting at which the land was distributed, for they anticipated the disputes among the various ethnic groups.

🍵 *View of Yunnan tea growing areas*

Angry as she was, Yao Bai was afraid that they would be badly off later without land. So she scattered a handful of seeds down from a mountain top. From that time, tea trees grew in Longpa Village, where the Jinuos started to plant and use tea. The high mountain where they lived became one of the six tea mountains of Yunnan Province. The story about Yao Bai's planting tea brought a history of tea planting to the first stage of human civilization.

Most tea historians hold that people successively used tea as herbs, food, and drink. The Jinuos have regarded tea as a "cold dish in sauce" to the present day. When you come to their villages, they will collect fresh tea leaves at once, crumple and knead them into soft and thin pieces, put them in a large bowl, and add some yellow fruit juice, sour bamboo shoots, sour ants, garlic, chili, and salt. Then they will ask you to taste their special "cold dish in sauce."

The Jinuos have regarded tea as a "cold dish in sauce" to the present day.

Tea is roasting in pots

Some ethnic groups, such as the Yi, Bai, Wa and Lahu, have the habit of drinking "roast tea." This type of tea is roasted in pots or bamboo tubes, or on steel plates. For example, the Lahus roast tea by shaking an earthenware pot on a burning stove. When the tea turns brown, they pour boiling water into the pot. The tea roasted in this way gives off a rich fragrant smell. The Wa ethnic group roasts tea on a thin steel plate, and then puts the roasted tea into a pot and pours in boiling water. The Bais have a way of roasting tea similar to that of the Lahus except that they add condiments such as sugar and puffed rice to the tea. They also endow the tea with cultural meaning such as sweetness first, bitterness second, and recollections last.

145

The bamboo tube tea, which is popular among some ethnic groups in Yunnan Province, is also noteworthy. Perhaps this tea is a transition from loose tea to lump tea by pressing against the cooking utensil while roasting. The bamboo tube tea of the Dai people is an example. When you climb into a bamboo building of the Dais, a girl in a tight skirt with a silver belt greets you at once, and the oldest man treats you to the bamboo tube tea. The girl puts tea leaves into a new, fragrant bamboo tube, and the elderly man places it onto a tripod on the stove to soften, evaporate, and roast the tea indirectly instead of scorching it. In about six to seven minutes, the tea-maker will press the tea leaves in the bamboo tube with a stick, stuff in raw tea leaves, and continue to roast until the bamboo tube is filled. After the tea leaves get dry, the tube is cut open and the cylinder-shaped bamboo tube tea leaves are ready. By breaking off some dry tea leaves, putting them into a bowl, and pouring some boiling water, the host can treat you to a bowl of tea with the fragrance of both bamboo and roasted tea leaves. From the process of producing roasted tea, we can see the custom of roasting tea left over by the Tang Dynasty, and the original form of "lump tea processed by pressing" as well. The round tea cake, popular in the Yangtze River in the Tang Dynasty, perhaps evolved from the roast tea of boundary ethnic groups, who processed tea

The bamboo tube tea of Yunnan

with the natural and primitive tools of bamboo tubes, while people in the central plains processed tea by pressing with molds.

From the above-mentioned examples, we can see the original forms of processing tea either by roasting and pressing and the use of it as a vegetable. Tea arose in the Yunnan-Guizhou plateau, entered Sichuan Province along the Yangtze River, and then reached Hunan and Hubei provinces through the Three Gorges. People in tea's original growing area must have had a special method of processing. The sour-ant cold tea in sauce made by the boundary people was followed by tea used by people

Anhua brick-shaped tea of Hunan

Pu'er brick-shaped tea of Yunan

in the central plains as vegetables; tea roasted by the boundary people in pots or bamboo tubes or on steel plates was followed by tea roasted by Lu Yu and tea roasted after evaporation; the cylinder-shaped tea roasted and pressed in bamboo tubes was followed by the perforated tea of the Tang Dynasty, the cake-shaped tea of the Song and Yuan dynasties, and the present-day brick-shaped tea and bowl-shaped tea.

In 633, Tibetan King Songzan Gambo put down a rebellion in northern Tibet. To strengthen contact with the central plains, he sent an envoy to the capital, Chang'an (today's Xi'an) to request unity by marriage in the year 641, the 15th year of the Zhenguan period of the Tang Dynasty. The Tang Emperor Taizong decided to marry his daughter, Princess Wencheng, to Songzan Gambo. When she went to Tibet, Princess Wencheng took many craftsmen and materials, which were said to include 3,800 kind of seeds, as well as skills of metallurgy, spinning and weaving, silk reeling, papermaking, and winemaking. In addition, she introduced the custom of tea drinking as social function to Tibet. In the Tang Dynasty, when tea culture came into being in the central plains, many people went to Tibet with methods of tea drinking and tea ceremonies and culture. *Jia,* the name used for tea in the Tang Dynasty in some parts of China, has been used in Tibetan culture, which shows that Tibetans started to drink tea early in the Tang Dynasty.

Princess Wencheng

In the book *Supplement to the History of the Tang* are the words: "Once, Duke Changlu was sent to Tibet as an envoy. When he was making tea in his tent, the Tibetan king asked him what he was making. Duke Changlu said, 'It is tea, which can remove worry as well as thirst.' The king said that he also had tea. Then Duke Changlu asked him to show his tea. The king put out his tea of various kinds, and pointed at the tea with his fingers, saying, 'This is Shouzhou tea, this is Shuzhou tea, this is Guzhu tea, this is Qimen tea, and this is Changming tea.'" This shows that the royal Tibetan court knew a great deal about the tea of the Central Plains during

Figurines depicting Princess Wencheng's journey to Tibet

the 200 years after Princess Wencheng went to Tibet. South of the Tibetan mountain areas, a popular folk song entitled *Princess Brings the Dragon-Design Tea Cup*, says, "The dragon-design teacup was brought into Tibet by Princess Wencheng. It reminds us of her kindly face." This shows that Princess Wencheng brought to Tibet not only tea leaves, but also tea sets. The tea cakes, popular in the Tang Dynasty, were further changed into those with the delicate design of a dragon or phoenix, which were brought into Tibet by Princess Wencheng. The Tibetans also believe that Princess Wencheng taught them how to grind and boil tea. Whenever they treat their guests to tea, they will tell how Princess Wencheng taught the ancient Tibetan women to make tea. Though songs and stories about her tend to be exaggerated, Princess

Wencheng is nevertheless held in high regard by Chinese tea historians.

In the development of tea culture of the central plains, Buddhism played an important role. Tibetan Buddhist culture attaches importance to tea ceremonies during Buddhist activities. Monks associate tea with meditation. When praying to deities in temples, they take tea with them. In the Zuglakhang Monastery in Lhasa, brick tea over one hundred years

🍵 *Tibetan tea sets*

old was collected, which, though actually useless as a drink, was treated by the monks as a treasure to protect the temple. Therefore, the Tibetans think of tea as something more holy and less utilitarian than the Han Chinese do.

Regarded as something pure and holy granted by Buddha, tea drinking in Tibetan temples requires a very solemn ceremony. More than 200 years ago, a Portuguese missionary wrote *My Travels from Tartary to Tibet* in which he gave a detailed description of the tea culture in Tibetan temples. The Tibetans, he wrote, have a surprising way of drinking tea. The tea bricks were of high quality, and five such tea bricks were valued at one tael of silver. All the teapots were made of silver. The teapots and teacups on golden saucers on the sacrificial altar in the Lama temple, which were all made of emerald, were beautiful to behold. In particular, the Kewenbamu Lamasery, which was the religious and cultural center of Tibet, was a most magnificent structure, attracting many scholars and pilgrims from all parts of China. The devout pilgrims treated the Lamas to tea. It took a lot of money to hold such a simple but momentous activity. Each of the 4,000 Lamas drank two cups of tea, which cost 56 taels of silver. The ceremony of presenting tea to Lamas was also a surprise. Some young men held a steaming hot boiler for the benefactors kneeling on the ground to give to the countless rows of Lamas in solemn robes who sat still. At this time the benefactors would sing hymns. Pilgrims would serve tea with refreshments.

🍵 *Tea making by Buddhist Lamas of Tibet*

149

From this we can see the following points:

1. Tea is vested with mystery in Tibetan temples. It has more spiritual meaning than material meaning. The Buddhists and Taoists on the central plains drink tea mainly to cultivate their moral character by sitting in meditation. They connect tea drinking with Buddhist or Taoist activities.

2. Tibetan temples are particular about tea art. Their teasets, for example, are not inferior to those of rich Han families, though they are no match for the royal court of the central plains. The tea, contained in boilers, is served in combination with the charity of the temples, as Tibetan tea culture not only absorbs the idea of charity in the tea culture of the central plains, but also contains the strong influence of Buddhism.

3. The tea ceremonies of Tibetan temples, grand, solemn, and large in scale, are different from those of the Tang Dynasty monks in the central plains, who decocted and boiled tea in all manner of settings both large and small. The large-scale Tibetan tea gathering was perhaps influenced in part by the large-scale

🍵 *Tibetan tea sets in carrying cases*

tea parties of temples in the Song Dynasty, or created by the Tibetans. Unlike the monks of the central plains, who drink tea to achieve peace of mind and find their true selves, the Buddhists of the Tibetan temples treat the tea they drink as something holy and miraculous bestowed on them by the spirits. This clearly shows their objective idealism, greatly different to reformed Chinese Buddhism, is more similar to the original form of Indian Buddhism.

Unlike some upper-class Tibetans, who drink Maojian tea or Yaxi tea, the common Tibetans and Lamas mainly drink Kangzhuan tea, Fuzhuan tea, Jinjian tea and Fangbao tea. Buttered tea and green tea are enjoyed in both pastoral and agricultural areas, where milky tea is also popular.

Milky tea is the Tibetans' main drink with rice or bread. The Tibetans generally drink several bowls of milky tea in the morning. They drink it five or six more times during the

150

course of the day. Milky tea is not only for daily use, but also for the reception of guests. Whenever a distinguished guest comes, Tibetans make mellow milky tea. First, they pound brick tea into pieces, and put them into the teapot to boil. Then they pour the hot, fragrant tea into a wooden vat over one meter high, put in some butter and salt, and mix with a stick. At this time, the tea, water, butter, and salt are dissolved. Then heating the tea in the teapot again, they finally get fragrant buttered tea. When a distinguished guest comes, they often present *hada* (a piece of white silk used as a gift among the Tibetans) to the guest, let him take a seat, and then offer the guest buttered tea. The Tibetans have a strong sense of etiquette when drinking milky tea. The host must continually add milky tea to the guest's bowl after he drinks, while the guest must, instead of drinking up the bowl of tea at one gulp, always leave half a bowl of the tea for the host to refill. If the host fills up the guest's bowl, the guest, upon leaving, must drink up the bowl at one gulp to express his thanks and satisfaction to the host.

151

Tibetan herdsmen are very hospitable. When a close friend or a new guest comes into one of their tents, the host, after bowing, immediately serves milky tea. Then the host puts ginseng, rice, steamed stuffed buns and other food on a plate, which is covered with *hada* to show respect for the guest. The most honored guest can use his hands to take meat and stewed vegetables.

For Tibetans, tea implies friendship, respect, purity and auspiciousness.

After tea arose in Yunnan and Guizhou provinces, it gradually began to be used in other places. It was largely used in two ways. One way was that it was used as a medicinal herb, a practice which then evolved into a tea cultural system, in which tea was consumed without other snacks or refreshments. For instance, various schools of tea culture in the central plains of China, such as

🍵 *Milky tea is the Tibetans' main drink*

the Taoist tea culture, the Buddhist tea culture, and the Confucian tea culture, which was the mainstay of the tea cultures, along with the people of Korea, Japan, and other countries in Southeast Asia influenced by the traditions of Confucian culture, all drank tea without refreshments. The other way was that tea was used as food, whence evolved a systematic tea culture in which tea was served with refreshments. For example, people south of the Yangtze River drink tea to go with condiments, while people in the northwest part of China and in some countries in Western Europe drink buttered tea or milky tea to go with brown sugar. It is reasonable for some people to hold that the culture of the northwest grasslands can be called the "milky tea culture," a title which reflects the connection between the life style of the people of northwest China, who made a living by grazing and hunting and who fed on a diet high in protein, and the mountain or forest farming culture.

In some sense, tea played an life changing role for herdsmen and hunters after it spread to China's steppes, grasslands, and pasture lands. It is often said that people make a living according to given circumstances. On high mountains and grasslands in the northwest part of China, a large quantity of cattle, sheep, camels, and horses are raised. The milk and meat provide people with much fat and protein but few other vitamins. Tea, therefore, supplements the basic needs of the nomadic tribes, whose diet lacks vegetables. Therefore, the herdsmen from the Qinghai-Tibet Plateau and the Xinjiang and Inner Mongolia autonomous regions follow the tea culture system, in which they drink tea with milk, and make milky tea the most precious thing for the people in the northwest part of China.

In the Xinjiang Uygur Autonomous Region, each person consumes approximately 500 grams of brick tea annually on average. The herdsmen eat tea leaves while they drink tea. Many ethnic groups in the region cannot go without pan cakes of wheat or corn flour, or milky tea when they have meals or receive guests. For the Hui minority, tea symbolizes purity apart from a daily necessity.

The Mongolian grasslands are full of a rich flavor of fragrant milky tea. In spite of their frequent removal on their felted carts to where grass is luxuriant, the Mongols never forget to boil milky tea. They first pound brick tea to pieces, then pour in water and boil the tea, filter the dregs, add the appropriate amount of milk, continue to boil, and frequently ladle out some tea before pouring it. The system is much like Lu Yu's way of making tea. The guests should not drink the tea up at one gulp, but allow the hostess to continually add tea to their bowls, in the same way as they drink buttered tea. The herdsmen generally add salt when they drink milky tea, but when treating guests to tea they add white sugar and salt to show their special respect. The stir-fried millet, called broom corn millet by the Mongols, is hard to chew. Large cakes of milky beancurd, resembling big cakes of soap, were hung out on the tents to dry. Whenever they entertain guests, the herdsmen cut the milky beancurd into square pieces, and let the guests eat it with white sugar. Milk, milky beancurd, and stir-fried millet are often difficult to digest, and vegetables are scarce on the grasslands, so tea often serves as the dietary solution which can aid digestion and increase the body's absorption of vitamins. The stir-fried millet is not often eaten, except for on long journeys or for the entertainment of guests. Milky tea thus becomes the Mongolians' main source of nutrition.

153

On the Mongolian grasslands, milky tea is used not only in daily life and the entertainment of guests, but also in grand festivals. For example, after the Mongolians ask Lamas to chant scriptures, they present them with *hada* and several pieces of brick tea. In autumn, at temple fairs or the Nadam Fair, people will entertain customers with milky tea, and brick tea

Scene of the Mongolian grasslands

Tea and Chinese Culture

is of course on sale in large quantities.

Like the Mongols, the Manchus of the Qing Dynasty came from the non-Han ethnicity from China's northeast. The Nüzhens started to drink tea early in the Liao and Kin (1115-1234) dynasties. Whenever a son-in-law called on his wife's family, all females of the family, young or old, would sit on the kang to receive him. Then the bride's family would warmly entertain him with tea, liquor, and candied fruit, etc. The Nüzhens called food served on festivals and food served to guests "tea food," which showed the role that tea played in their life.

Din Guanpeng: Nüzhens (Qing Dynasty)

With the rise of the Manchus, it became a common practice for the northern ethnic groups to drink tea. And the descendants of the Nüzhens still enjoyed drinking tea. After the reign of Emperor Qianlong, Emperors were addicted to tea, making it popular with the Manchus.

Transporting tea

Chapter 10

10. *Imperial Tea Culture*

The Manchus made outstanding contributions to tea culture. First, the Manchus organically connected the tea culture that was characterized by serving tea without refreshments and the tea culture characterized by serving tea with refreshments, and they put the milky tea culture to a position almost equal with that characterized by serving tea without refreshments. In the Qing Dynasty, Emperors and empresses liked to eat dairy products and drink milky tea. At the Elders' Banquet, which started at the time of Emperor Kangxi, the

officials in charge of tea and meals first presented a cup of brown milky tea to the Emperor and his sons, respectively. After the Emperor and the royal princes drank the milky tea, the officials presented tea senior to ministers. This shows that the Manchu Emperors had inherited the northern practice of drinking milky tea. The introduction of milky tea to the imperial court affirmed the important position of tea culture characterized by serving tea with refreshments. According to *Records from the Yangji House,* the Manchus used to drink milky tea. Rules were made to provide cows for the Emperor and his officials. Milk was sent to the tea house for boiling, and milky cakes were made in the tea house in spring and autumn. The herdsmen and hunters on grasslands liked to drink tea to go with milk, while the Nüzhens used to drink tea along with all manner of refreshments. It can be seen from this that the Manchus had three sources of tea culture: first, since the Liao and Jin dynasties they had adopted the northwest ethnic groups' custom of drinking milky tea; second, they followed the Nüzhens' custom of drinking tea to go with fruits and refreshments; third, they inherited the Han custom of drink-

Duomu pot for milky tea (Qing Dynasty)

ing tea without refreshments. Emperor Qianlong drank milky tea both at court in his daily life and at banquets; but when he was present at tea banquets or was composing poems or painting pictures, he became a bosom friend of Confucian tea drinkers, for in such situations he liked to drink tea without refreshments. Thus, the Manchus drew together the tea customs of ethnic groups of the Central Plains, the northwest, and the northeast.

Most Chinese tea-drinkers advocate the Confucian-inspired method of tea drinking, that is, the drinking of tea without refreshments rather than drinking tea with refreshments or drinking milky tea. However, the tea culture characterized by drinking tea with refreshments plays a noticeable role not only in China but throughout the world. According to statistics, 1. 3-1.5 billion people in the world drink tea without refreshments, while 100 million Chinese and 3.8-4.0 billion people from other countries drink tea with refreshments. At present, most typical tea houses in Beijing sell both tea and refreshments, leaving it up to the customer to decide what he or she wants.

As the imperial family of the Qing Dynasty liked to drink scented tea, semi-fermented tea (a sort of scented tea between black tea and green tea) developed rapidly. Semi-fermented tea pushed forward the changing of Chinese tea culture. The "Eight Banners" (military-administrative organizations of the Manchus in the Qing Dynasty), combined tea with flowers and created many kinds of tea, undoubtedly enriching Chinese tea culture.

Teacups with lids were popular with the imperial family of the Qing Dynasty. As the Manchus lived in a cold are in the northeast of China, it was necessary for them to keep the tea in the teacups warm with lids. The lids keep the tea warm and clean, help dispel tea leaves, and can be used to cover the mouth while drinking so as to show respect for others.

The common Manchu people often treated guests to tea at home. In all, the Manchus played an important role in the combination of the tea cultures of all ethnic groups, as well as in the development of tea art and tea ceremonies in China.

Teacup with lid (Qing Dynasty)

The Forbidden City was the imperial palace of the Ming and Qing Dynasties. The tea served there was for the Emperor and was a tribute from the tea-growing provinces to the south. It was kept in the palace and stored for future use. The excellence and quality of this tea was often beyond description. Numerous tea parties were held in the palace, presided over by the Emperor and his most senior ministers.

The Forbidden City

Most tea parties in the Forbidden City were held in Wenhua Hall (the Hall of Literary Glory), Chonghua Palace (the Hall of Double Glory) or Qianqing Palace (the Hall of Heavenly Purity). Upon entering the Meridian Gate of the Imperial Palace, one came to the Gate of Supreme Harmony. East of the Gate of Supreme Harmony was an external courtyard that contained three buildings: The main hall, called the Hall of Literary Glory, was in front; the Hall of Main Respect was in the middle; and the Imperial Library was in the rear. It was in these buildings that the Qing Dynasty Emperors honored Confucius, listened to lectures with

Qianqing Palace (the Hall of Heavenly Purity)

their ministers, and kept the imperial book collection. This area was the cultural center of the Forbidden City, and tea was served whenever the Emperors attended lectures.

As early as the Ming Dynasty, it became an important rite for tea to be served in the Hall of Literary Glory whenever the Emperors listened to lectures. The Ming Dynasty emperors and their ministers attended lectures in this hall three times a month. A lecturer spoke first about literature, then about classics, and last about history. After the lecture, the Emperor gave tea to the lecturer and his ministers. Tea was served so the lecturer could moisten his throat, but more importantly, it was seen as a symbolic gesture by the Emperor to encourage the process of education and learning.

The system of lecturing the emperors in the Hall of Literary Glory continued into the Qing Dynasty, but the ceremony became even grander. Emperor Qianlong attended 49 grand lectures, each including a spectacular ceremony. When the Emperor arrived, he was saluted by all his officials. The lecture began with four officials of the Manchu and Han nationalities talking about the Four Books of Confucius (*The Analects*, *The Great*

161

The Four Books of Confucius by Zhu Xi of Ming Dynasty

Learning, *The Doctrine of the Mean*, and *Mencius*). Then the Emperor expounded on the books and all officials had to listen while still on their knees. This was followed further still by a lecture in the same style on the Five Classics (the *Book of Changes*, the *Book of Songs*, the *Book of History*, the *Book of Rites*, and the *Spring and Autumn Annals*).

After the lectures, the Emperor asked those present to sit and have tea. Unlike a picnic or a chat in a tea house, tea was served in a solemn atmosphere not only in the palace, but also in the Confucian Temple and in the Imperial Academy. The Emperor also presented tea to officials whenever he made inspections. This showed that the tea offered by the Emperor, apart from his wine and gift giving, was a symbol to promote Confucian doctrine and ethics, and to encourage education.

The Spring and Autumn Annals

The Emperor also gave a grand "tea banquet" in Chonghua Palace (the Hall of Double Glory) in the Forbidden City almost every year during the Qing Dynasty.

Tea parties were first described in the Tang Dynasty. Large tea parties were also held in the palace during the Song Dynasty, with the Emperor serving the tea. Cai Jing (1047-1126), a prime minister serving under the Song Dynasty, described how the Emperor served tea to him as well as the princes in the Palace of Yanfu. He said the Emperor ordered his personal attendant to take the tea sets, and then personally poured boiling water into the cups of his guests. The guests all bowed in gratitude.

Emperor Qianlong of the Qing Dynasty was a tea lover and a great tea drinker. It is said that he wanted to retire from his throne in his late years, and some ministers, alarmed, asked: "How can a nation be without an Emperor even for a single day?" Qianlong replied with a smile: "How can the Emperor be without tea for a single day?" The Chonghua Palace was Qianlong's former residence before he ascended to the throne, and was called the palace after he became Emperor.

Besides being an avid tea drinker, Qianlong was an avid poet. He held tea parties in the palace, following the examples of earlier rulers. This became the annual tea dinner held in the Qing palace. It was held on a lucky day chosen between the 2nd and 10th days of the first lunar month. Everyone was to write poems while drinking tea. Initially, the number of people present was not fixed. They were mostly court officials who specialized in literature. Later, the Emperor selected a topic about which the participants wrote poems. Only the long poems were recited. Finally, it was decided the poems should have 72 rhymes, and only 18 people were invited to attend the tea party. They were divided into eight rows and each person wrote four lines. Qianlong personally chose the topic and made it known beforehand, but he only gave the beginning rhymes when

162

🍵 *Teapot with enamel painting (Qing dynasty)*

the party began in order to keep the officials guessing.

When the poems had been completed, Qianlong immediately read them one after another, then bestowed cups of tea and awarded prizes. Those who received awards carried the prizes out of the palace themselves to display their glory. Inviting 18 people to attend the tea party followed the example set by Emperor Taizong of the Tang Dynasty, who selected 18 literati from all over the nation to live and work in the Hall of Literature.

Following Qianlong, succeeding emperors also gave tea parties in Chonghua Palace, but none matched their illustrious predecessor. Most of the poems composed at these tea parties offered words of praise and flattery. Moreover, in the depths of the heavily guarded palace and in the presence of the Emperor, it was impossible for the literati to mix tea with poetry, man with nature, or their inner world with an objective frame of mind. Nevertheless, the relationship between tea and cultural circles was strengthened through the tea parties, and helped link tea with art at the highest levels of government.

The largest tea party ever held during the Qing Dynasty was held in the Palace of Heavenly Purity and was attended by more than one thousand people. The Ming Dynasty emperors had used the Palace of Heavenly Purity as sleeping quarters, but this changed during the Qing Dynasty. The Qing emperors used it to handle national affairs, summon ministers and officials, meet common people, hold palace ceremonies, receive foreign envoys, read books and memorials, and give comments and instructions to ministers and bureaucrats.

During their respective reigns, Emperor Kangxi and Emperor Qianlong held large banquets for more than 1,000 people in the Palace of Heavenly Purity. These banquets had the largest attendance with the highest ranking officials in the history of tea culture.

The 52nd year of Kangxi's Reign (1713) coincided with his 60th birthday. Local officials throughout the country encouraged their local elders to travel to the capital to congratulate the Emperor on his birthday. Emperor Kangxi, therefore, decided to hold a "Banquet of a Thousand Elders." He gave the banquet in the Garden of Flourishing Spring rather than in the palace, and more than 1,800 people were in attendance.

An important part of the banquet naturally involved tea drinking. The banquet began with everyone taking his seat for tea. The imperial musicians played, and the princes, dukes, and ministers saluted when the officials of the Imperial Kitchen presented cups of black tea with milk to the Emperor. After the Emperor finished, he invited his guests to drink as well. They received the tea sets afterward, and they all bowed in gratitude when they received the cups. After the ceremonies were completed, they began to eat.

Qianlong held two other banquets of this kind. In the first month of the 50th year of his reign, Qianlong gave a banquet in the Palace of Heavenly Purity for more than 3,000 elders. The eldest was aged 104 years. In order to attend the banquet, many people came to Beijing weeks in advance of the event.

In the 61st year of his reign, Qianlong gave another large banquet for more than 3,000 people in the Hall of Imperial Models. Another 5,000 people were invited but did not have seats. Ministers of the first rank were inside the hall. Officials of the second rank and foreign envoys were under the eaves. Officials of the third rank were on the steps and passage to the throne. Officials of the fourth and fifth rank and Mongolian officials were below and around the steps, and all others were outside the Gate of Peace and Longevity.

There were 800 tables arranged on two sides – east and west – six rows on each side. The shortest row had 22 tables; the longest had 100. There were too many people to receive the Emperor's tea service; so tea kitchen officials presented tea to the Emperor on behalf of all those present. Those who drank tea received a tea set while those who drank wine received a wine set.

The Qing Palace blended tea drinking with political and cultural activities in five ways:

1. Tea drinking ceremonies were used to honor Confucius, inspect the Imperial Academy, and listen to lectures. The ceremonies were used to link tea with Confucianism, distinguish the Emperor, and preach ethics, ideology and education.

2. Tea drinking was combined with poetry and cultural affairs meetings to promote culture. As an example, Emperor Qianlong combined tea drinking with writing poetry, compiling the Four Collections of Books.

3. Tea drinking was used at birthday celebrations, national festivities, and congratulatory occasions. In Chinese tea culture, literati, Taoists, and Buddhists stressed poverty, honesty, and retreat from public life while the imperial court and the common people stressed joy,

gaiety, and festivity. Tea parties held in the Qing Palace pushed the latter three to new heights.

4. The tea served at the "1,000 Elders' Banquets" in the Qing Dynasty was black tea with milk. The Royal Family drank black tea with milk in their everyday life. The number of dairy cows supplying milk to the court was fixed by decree. The milk was delivered to the director of the Tea Kitchen. The Tea Kitchen made milk cakes during the spring and autumn seasons. Those in the imperial court drank both clear tea and tea with milk.

Originally, people in the northern part of China drank milk tea, and the drinking of milk tea in the Qing court was at first intended to maintain health. However, at the "1,000 Elders' Banquet" the tea served by the Emperor added the color of the northern ethnic minorities to the existing tea culture. It shows that China's tea culture was sympathetic to the blending of China's different nationalities—politically, socially, and culturally. All of China's ethnic minorities recognized tea as a cultural concept and it was not exclusive to the Han (or majority) ethnic group.

5. Tea culture activities in the Qing palace flourished during Qianlong's reign, the greatest tea connoisseur of all the emperors. Between the 8th and 60th years of his reign, Qianlong gave tea banquets every year for 48 years. During Qianlong's reign, the Qing economy was prosperous, the cultures of the Manchus and the Hans were well blended, and the arts flourished.

Strong tea is made when 3 or 4 grams of dry tea is mixed with one cup of boiling water. Strong tea may lead to insomnia in certain people, yet it can also be good for heart and lungs, and can be beneficial to those who smoke, drink, or eat too much.

🍵 *Teapot in the shape of root (Qing dynasty)*

Chapter 11

11. The Global Appeal of Chinese Tea

The spread of Chinese tea and tea culture to other Asian countries, especially to the empires of Japan and Korea, is notable. Societies in Korea and Japan, like China, have many detailed records about the spread of tea and tea culture. According to historical documents and cultural relics excavated, Chinese culture has influenced Korean and Japanese culture, including tea in both its material and spiritual and aesthetic forms.

In 593, in the reign of Emperor Wendi of the Sui Dynasty, China introduced tea to Japan along with the spread of its culture, art, and Buddhism. In 729, a grand tea celebration was held in the Japanese royal court. That day, the Japanese Emperor assembled 100 monks to expound the texts of Buddhism in the royal residence. The next day, the monks were given tea. Seventy five years later, the founder of the Japanese Tiantai (Tien-tai) Sect of Buddhism, came to China in 804 (the 20th year of Zhenyuan during the reign of Emperor Dezong of the Tang Dynasty). The next year (the first year of Yongzhen during the reign of Emperor Shunzong of the Tang Dynasty), he returned to his country carrying Buddhist scriptures and Chinese tea seeds, which were planted on a mountain near a river. Another Japanese monk came to China in 804, and returned to Japan in 806. He learned the Truth-Word Sect of Buddhism in Chang'an (today's Xi'an), the Tang capital. When he returned to Japan, he took with him tea seeds, a stone mortar with which to process tea, as well as the skills of processing tea by steaming, pounding and roasting. At that time, encouraged by the monks, the Japanese started to drink tea as people of the Tang Dynasty did. They boiled cake tea, and added such condiments as sweet kudzu vines and ginger. Owing to the limited quantity of tea trees planted, only the royal family and a small number of monks drank tea at the time.

The founder of the Japanese Tiantai Sect of Buddhism, Zui Chen

After the reign of Hirayasu, Japan made fewer contacts with China over almost 200 years from the Five Dynasties (907-960) to the Song and Liao dynasties. Chinese tea fell out of favor in Japan, and it was not until the Southern Song Dynasty that Japanese monk Eisai reintroduced tea into Japan.

When he was 14 years old, Eisai left home and was initiated into monkhood, studying in the Buddhist institute of the highest learning dedicated to the Japanese Tiantai sect. At the age of 21, he was determined to study in China. In the fourth year (1168) of Qiandao during the reign of Emperor Xiaozong of the Southern Song Dynasty, Eisai started off in Mingzhou Prefecture, Zhejiang Province, traveled through famous mountains and visited magnificent temples south of the Yangtze River, paid respects to Master Xu'an of the Chan Sect at the Longevity Temple on the Tiantai Mountain, and moved to

🍵 *The Japanese monk Eisai*

169

the Jingde Temple on the Tongshan Mountain with Master Xu'an. At that time tea drinking prevailed, and Eisai enjoyed the local customs. He lived in China for 24 years, and returned to Japan in 1192. Therefore, Eisai knew not only the general skills of Chinese tea art, but also the tea art of the Chan Sect. After he returned to Japan, Eisai personally planted tea trees, and wrote *Health Preserving by Drinking Tea,* which absorbed the ideas of *The Book of Tea* by Lu Yu, and specially stressed such functions of tea as health care and cultivation of one's moral character. Thus, Eisai was the real founder of the Japanese tea art.

In the Yuan and Ming dynasties, Japanese monks continued to come to China. In particular, eminent Japanese monks mastered the tea-drinking skills of both the Ming Buddhist monks and the scholars, combined their skills, and created the Japanese tea art, which started to reach perfection. It can be seen from the above that the Japanese introduced, and then, according to their own national traits, improved Chinese tea art and the skills of planting, producing and drinking tea. It is not, therefore, a surprise that the Japanese retained the ancient Chinese tea art and formed a branch of Chinese tea culture.

A Korean painting about tea

According to historical records, tea was introduced from China into Korea in around 632 to 646. From then on, the Chinese custom of drinking tea and Chinese tea art were introduced into Korea. On the tablet inscription for Master Zhenjian, an eminent Korean monk (755-850) who set up the Double Stream Temple in Korea, was written, "If the Chinese tea is received again, put it into a stone pot and boil it with firewood."

Drinking tea became a ceremony in Korean temples during this period. The book *Travels in the South* by a Korean writer, who mastered the skills of making tea, reads "I had intended to boil tea to present the revered Xiao, but found no spring water. Suddenly, the spring water in the rock crack gushed out, smelling sweet like milk. So I tried making tea with the spring water." It can be seen from this that Korean monks not only boiled tea in ceremonies, but also paid attention to tea art and the quality of water used to make tea. In 828, an envoy from Korea took tea seeds away with him from China.

From then on, the Koreans started to plant and produce tea. Currently, Korean tea production is more than 1.6 kilotons annually in about 3,300 acres of major tea plantations.

It is generally thought that Chinese tea was introduced into South Asia in the Northern and Southern Song dynasties. The Northern Song government established maritime tax supervisory boards in Guangzhou, Mingzhou, Hangzhou and Quanzhou. Tea was exported to Southeast Asia through Guangzhou, Quanzhou, and to Japan and Korea through Mingzhou.

In the Southern Song Dynasty, the Chinese tea trade expanded to India, Africa, central Asia, the Arabian Peninsula, and Europe. Foreign businessmen often traveled between Chinese ports cities. At that time, Quanzhou, a major port opening to foreign countries, had frequent trade contacts with several Asian and African countries. Tea produced in Fujian Province was sold abroad in large quantities. In particular, Fengming tea, produced in the Lotus Peak of Nan'an, became a major product exported to South Asia.

In the Ming Dynasty, admiral Zheng He made voyages to the Western world seven times, and traveled through the regions of Vietnam, Java, India, Sri Lanka, the Arabian Peninsula and the eastern coast of Africa, each time taking tea with him.

The countries of Southeast Asia not only imported Chinese tea, but also introduced from China the skills for planting tea. Tea planting began in Indonesia in the 16th century, with the major plantations in Sumatra. In 1684 and 1731, Chinese tea seeds were introduced into Southeast Asia in large quantities. The year 1731, in particular, witnessed a remarkable success in the germination rate.

Statue of Zheng He

Tea was introduced into northern India by Tibetan monks. It is estimated that Indians started to get some idea of the skills of drinking Chinese tea in the Tang and Song dynasties. In 1780 and 1788 the British East India Company imported some tea powder into India, which gradually became one of the largest tea-producing countries.

Ostindiefararen Götheborg

Mark of transports of the
British East India Company

It was of great importance that the countries of South Asia planted Chinese tea and formed the habit of drinking tea. This is because Chinese tea was exported by sea through these countries to the Mediterranean and European and African countries, and a tea route leading to the West developed after the Yuan and Ming dynasties. Through the countries of South Asia the Western countries imported the skills of planting and producing Chinese tea, produced large quantities of tea by virtue of the favorable natural conditions and the cheap labor force of Southeast Asia, and then transported the tea to Europe. This was much more convenient than the purchase of tea directly from China in the Ming Dynasty and the early Qing Dynasty. Therefore, the popularity of planting and drinking tea in South Asia not only reflected the extension of Chinese tea culture, but was also a prelude to the development and spread of Chinese tea culture towards the West.

Tea and Chinese Culture

The spread of Chinese tea to the West largely underwent three periods. The first period was during the Yuan Dynasty, when Genghis Khan mounted large scale expeditions deep into central Asia and Eastern Europe. Since Mongolia was very early the transport station for the tea of the Central Plains to spread to the Central and West Asia, the Mongols cannot have gone without taking milky tea with them far to Europe via West Asia on this expedition. Eastern Europe probably knew about Chinese tea in this period, and it is likely that the expedition was connected to the fact that Russians imported tea from China later.

🍵 *Marco Polo*

Naturally, there were some who gained information about Chinese tea on their own initiative. Chinese tea was seen in Western records in the Yuan Dynasty. Marco Polo, a famous Italian merchant and friend of Khublai Khan, came to China with his uncle, traveling through Central Asia, Xingjiang, the northwest grasslands, Shangdu, and Dadu. He stayed in China for more than ten years, and served as an official under the Yuan government. At that time, people kept tea cakes, which had been used since the Tang and Song dynasties, as well as loose tea and the skill of stirring tea. Marco Polo, who maintained frequent contacts with the Chinese people, cannot have been unaware of their custom of drinking tea. Over ten years later, he returned to his country as an envoy of the Yuan government. This time he made his way from the south, traveling through the tea towns south of the Yangtze River, the countries of South Asia, the Indian Ocean and the Mediterranean. It is unknown whether he presented tea as gifts to the countries he visited. The second period was during the Ming Dynasty, about the 16th century, when Chinese tea was exported on a small-scale and was gradually spread abroad.

In 1567, when Emperor Muzong of the Ming Dynasty ascended the throne, two men from southern Russia were said to have acquired Chinese tea and introduced it into Russia. In 1618, the Chinese ambassador in Russia presented a small amount of tea to the Tsar. In 1735, the trade caravans established during the reign of Empress Elizabeth traveled between China and Russia, and specially conveyed tea for the royal family, nobles and officials. Owing to the arduous transportation, the tea was expensive.

In 1607, Dutch ships reached Java, a Dutch colony. They arrived later in Macao to carry green tea, and then returned to Europe in 1610. This was the beginning of Western transport of tea from their colonies in the east, and the start of the importation of tea from China to Western Europe. In 1637, ships of the British East India Company transported tea from Guangzhou. At the same time, the China tea trade with the British empire began, culminating in the Canton Trade of the mid 18th century. Other countries such as Sweden, Holland, Denmark, France, Spain, Portugal, Germany, Hungary and others, transported huge amounts of tea from China each year.

 Contemporary western tea brand

In the 150 or so years which have marked the latter half of the 19th century and most of the 20th century, China has been subject to struggles and wars both internal and external. In many ways, as it has been throughout history, we have seen how tea culture can survive even during periods of societal disarray. Tea has remained the constant process, continually being enjoyed and consumed no matter what the situation.

Today, the aesthetic and health benefits of Chinese tea have worldwide appeal. Interest in tea as well as in tea culture remains at an all-time high by both amateurs and connoisseurs. In some part of the West, for example, tea has even surpassed coffee in popularity. Currently, tea is a multimillion dollar industry worldwide. People in every continent and in every hemisphere drink tea. Distilled down to its basic elements, however, tea is one of the purest, simplest aesthetic and artistic forms in the history of world food and drink. It has influenced philosophy, history, art, and culture for centuries. Each new generation to discover tea brings a fresh reassessment and reevaluation on how tea can fit into contemporary society. It is truly wondrous to see how this basic, aesthetically pure and simple concoction of water and tea, poured in a cup or teapot, can lift the spirit and raise the physical and psychological level of all those who enjoy tea and make it an important part of their lives.

Appendices

Appendix 1: Nutrition

Tea has been consumed in China for five thousand years. Scholars credit the discovery of tea leaves and their medicinal value to Shen Nong during Chinese antiquity.

Chaye (tea leaf) was called *ming* in ancient times. Shen Nong's discovery revealed that tea could treat illness. Over the millennia, tea has been found to contain hundreds of natural chemical properties and is an effective medicine for preventing and treating numerous illnesses and ailments. The evolution from using tea as a sacrifice to using it as a medicinal treatment and a relaxing drink is proof that its value to world history should not be underestimated.

Ancient Chinese medical texts thoroughly discuss the medicinal properties of tea. In *The Book of Tea*, Lu Yu concluded: "The use of tea as a drink started with Shen Nong." He also observed: "The more you drink tea, the more vigorous and refreshed you are."

In recent years, the chemical and nutritional properties of tea have been divided into two main categories: nutrients needed by the human body, and nonessential elements that improve the health in certain pathological conditions. The latter are referred to as "elements with medicinal effect." Descriptions of some of these chemicals follow:

The world's oldest tea tree is over 2,700 years old. It stands 108 feet tall, and is still growing. It is located in the Xishuangbanna forest of Yunnan Province.

Alkaloids. Tea contains purines, among which are caffeine and theophylline. The amount of caffeine varies greatly with the variety of tea. Caffeine dissolves in water. If someone drinks five to six cups of tea a day, about 0.3 grams of caffeine is absorbed. This amount is significant, but the caffeine is released through a diuretic process and does not remain in the human body. Caffeine and theophylline have similar pharmacological effects; they both stimulate the central nervous system. Caffeine can improve thinking, increase energy, and decrease drowsiness. Stimulation of the spinal cord helps strengthen the muscles and reduce fatigue. The caffeine in tea does not result in secondary depression or ill side effects. Theophylline works as a muscle relaxant and vasodilator, whereas caffeine is primarily a stimulant and diuretic.

Tea trees between 100 and 200 years old have the highest output of harvested tea.

Diuresis. Together, caffeine and theophylline are believed to produce diuresis. They dilate blood vessels in the kidneys so the kidneys excrete unnecessary water, and they stimulate the bladder to increase the amount of urine expelled by the body. For these reasons, tea drinking has some effect in treating cardiac edema as well as premenstrual syndrome.

Stimulation of the cardiac muscles. Tea stimulates the heart and strengthens the systolic process of the left ventricle, but how the tea is processed affects this ability. Unfermented green tea has the strongest effect, semi–fermented tea is less strong, and fermented black tea is the weakest in this regard.

Dilation of blood vessels. Longjing was found to lower serum cholesterol and reduce arteriosclerosis.

Digestion and breathing. Caffeine stimulates the secretion of hydrochloric acid, thereby aiding digestion.

Respiration. Caffeine relaxes the smooth muscle of the bronchus. Therefore, drinking tea helps control asthma.

Hormones. It is reported that theophylline can increase the production of female hormones.

Polyphenols. Tea polyphenols are also called Tannin, which stimulates the adrenal gland thereby increasing energy. It helps strengthen blood vessels and capillaries.

Anti–inflamatories. Tea helps improve the metabolism of vitamin C and the resistance and anti–inflammatory properties of capillaries. Foods high in vitamin C, together with green tea, have been found to increase the body's ability to resist infection (black tea, however, lacks this effect).

The increased ability to resist infection is caused by the combined effect of tea and vita-

177

min C. Tea protects vitamin C from being oxidized. Tea increases the accumulation of vitamin C in the liver, spleen, kidneys, intestines, brain, and blood, and thereby reduces the amount of vitamin C excreted in the urine.

Gargling with green tea can help one avoid the flu.

Antibiotic effect. Green tea inhibits the growth of salmonella typhus, dysentery bacilli, staphylococcus aureus, and vibrio cholera. Experiments in China have shown that tea inhibits and kills dysentery bacillus.

Ester polysaccharide. This is an important component in the cell walls of the tea leaves. Tea ester polysaccharides help prevent radioactive injuries, improve blood–building functions, and protect the blood.

Proteins and amino acids. Tea leaves contain both amino acids and proteins. The protein contained in black tea is 15-30% of its dry weight, but less than 2% dissolves in water. Cow's milk added to tea reduces the astringency of tea, but does not block the absorption of protein. Black tea contains few amino acids, but green tea contains 16 to 24 amino acids, including cystine (a major metabolic sulfur source), serine, and theophyllamine acid. Of these three amino acids, theophyllamine acid is unique to tea, and accounts for 50% of the total amino acids in tea. Almost all amino acids needed by the human body are found in tea.

Sugar. Tea is low in calories. The sugar obtained from tea made in boiling water is only 4–5%. However, drinking tea increases the body's absorption of sugar. If milk and sugar are added to tea, and someone drinks six cups a day, the calories obtained from tea will equal 7–10% of an adult's daily caloric requirements.

Fat. Fat accounts for about 2–3% of the weight of processed black tea.

Vitamins. Tea contains vitamins A, B, C, E, and K, all of which are essential to the human body. Generally, green tea contains more vitamins than black tea. Black tea and green tea contain roughly the same B vitamins, but their composition and content vary by region due to different cultivating and processing conditions.

Minerals. Tea contains many minerals. Fresh tea leaves and black tea contain about 4–9% minerals, most of which are needed by the human body. The quantity of minerals contained in tea grown in different parts of the world differs. Russian scholars report that tea does not contain much iron and copper, so tea has limited effectiveness in curing anemia. Tea contains little sodium and so is a good drink for those suffering from hypertension. Tea plants are apt to accumulate manganese, aluminum, and fluorine, as well as other elements.

Aromatic compounds. Tea leaves contain aromatic matter. These volatile compounds account for 0.6% of the dry weight of the tea leaves. Using tea liquid to rinse the mouth helps remove grease, strengthen the teeth, and prevent halitosis.

Selenium. Selenium was recognized by Chinese scientists in 1973 as one of the 14 elements indispensable to human life. The amount of selenium in tea varies by region; in some places it is very high. As selenium is a strong antioxidant and protects the cell membranes, it can help prevent cancer and other diseases, and it has no side effects. Some scientists have argued that the selenium extraction rate from tea is as low as 20% to 40% and, therefore, is insufficient to make up for a selenium deficiency. However, it is believed that the extraction rate can be raised. Tea bags and instant tea raise the extraction rate to 60-80%. Moreover, eating food with tea also helps raise the extraction rate.

179

🍵 *Old people like to enjoy tea in their leasure time*

Appendix 2: A Brief Chinese Chronology

Xia Dynasty			C. 2100-C. 1600 B.C.
Shang Dynasty			C. 1600-C. 1100 B.C.
Zhou Dynasty	Western Zhou Dynasty		C. 1100-771 B.C.
	Eastern Zhou Dynasty Spring And Autumn Period Warring States Period		770-256 B.C. 770-476 B.C. 475-221 B.C.
Qin Dynasty			221-206 B.C.
Han Dynasty	Western Han		206 B.C.-25 A.D.
	Eastern Han		25-220 A.D.
Three Kingdoms	Wei		220-265
	Shu Han		221-263
	Wu		222-280
Western Jin Dynasty			265-316
Eastern Jin Dynasty			317-420
Northern and Southern Dynasty	Southern Dynasty	Song	420-479
		Qi	479-502
		Liang	502-557
		Chen	557-589
	Northern Dynasty	Northern Wei	386-534
		Eastern Wei	534-550
		Nortern Qi	550-577

		Western Wei	535-556
		Nortern Zhou	557-581
Sui Dynasty			581-618
Tang Dynasty			618-907
Five Dynasties		Later Liang	907-923
		Later Tang	923-936
		Later Jin	936-947
		Later Han	947-950
		Later Zhou	951-960
Song Dynasty		Northern Song Dynasty	960-1127
		Southern Song Dynasty	1127-1279
Liao Dynasty			916-1125
Kin Dynasty			1115-1234
Yuan Dynasty			1271-1368
Ming Dynasty			1368-1644
Qing Dynasty			1644-1911
Republic of China			1912-1949
People's Republic of China			1949-

181

Appendix 3: Famous Chinese Teas

Main Types(Based on processing difference and different characteristics)	Green Teas (nonfermentted, or nonoxidized)	Xihu Longjing Taiping Houkui Guzhu Zisun Gaoqiao Yinfeng Jiukeng Maojian Jingting Luxue Tianmu Qingding Xinyang Maojian Liu'an Guapian Laozhu Dafang Pingshui Zhucha Anhua Songzhen Qiangang Huibai Dongting Biluochun Putuo Focha Nanjing Yuhuacha Huading Yunwu Weishan Baimaojian Lushan Yunwu Tunlu Wuyuan Mingmei Mengding Xueshui Yunlu Huiming Huangshan Maofeng
	White Teas (slightly fermented)	Yinzhen Baihao Baimudan Gongmei
	Yellow Teas (slightly fermented)	Wenzhou Huangtang Junshan Yinzhen Mengding Huangya Mogan Huangya Beifang Maojiaz Luyuan Maojian Huoshan Huangcha Guangdong Dayeqing

	Oolong Teas (semifermented)	Wuyi Yancha Da Hongpao Shuixian Rougui Anxi Tieguanyin Qilan	Huangjingui Fenghuang Dancong Fenghuang Shuixian Lingtou Dancong Taiwan Baozhong Taiwan Wulong
	Red Teas (fermented)	Jiuqu Hongmei Zhengshan Xiaozhong Dianhong Qihong	Ninghong Yingde Hongcha Bailin Gongfucha
	Black Teas (fermented)	Anhua Heicha Puqi Laoqingcha Yunnan Pu'ercha Yunnan Tuocha Cangwu Liubaocha	
Re-processed Teas	Scented Teas	Moli Huacha Zhulan Huacha Meigui Huacha Guihuacha	
	Scented Teas	Lizhi Hongcha Ningmeng Hongcha Mihoutao Cha	
	Compressed Teas	Tuocha Pu'er Fangcha Xiangjian Cha	Heizhuan Cha Fangbao Cha Liubao Cha

183